Don't Believe the HYPErtension

Edie,

Love it that you "get"
my sense of humor. Hope
you enjoy the book and figure
out who I'm talking about.

Take care,
Tom Schuli

Don't Believe the HYPErtension

Surviving Aortic Dissection and Other Stuff

R.A. Fields

To order additional copies of this book, contact:
Xlibris
1-888-795-4274
www.Xlibris.com
Orders@Xlibris.com
766654

Contents

INTRODUCTION

WHEN I WAS a child, I had two choices for my career. The first was to play center field for the New York Yankees. If that dream fell through, my second choice was to become a park ranger for a national park and spend my days in a ranger tower, scouting for forest fires. The first dream ended at college. The latter never materialized. My career, for the past thirty years, has been that of a groundskeeper, with a few odd jobs mixed in along the way. As I begin this endeavor (writing this book), I recently turned fifty and quit my latest job as an athletic-field groundskeeper for a college in Virginia. Near my home here, there is a quiet, beautiful two-mile walk around a small lake. During these walks, my mind begins to retrieve stories from my youth and professional life. The following pages are a look into my world and some of the crazy things that have shaped me into the person I am.

GROWING UP

I GREW UP as the middle child of five, in a small town in southern New Jersey. Two older sisters and a younger brother and sister made getting attention from at least one parent very challenging, to say the least. It was a great town to grow up in. The school system didn't have busing. Every child was close enough to school to walk, so riding on a school bus to go on a field trip or a high school sporting event was a huge deal. My father was the only son of a Pennsylvania coal miner, and he had served in WWII during the battle of Saipan. He held down two jobs, while my mother raised the five children. He was a schoolteacher during the day and a member of the butchers' union at night. At best, he had two hours at home between jobs during the week.

In the summer of 1975, the movie *Jaws* hit theaters. Everyone I knew was seeing it. Remember, this was long before video games, the internet, and even cable TV. I do not know what my parents were thinking when they decided to take the family. My youngest sibling, my sister, was six or seven at the time, and she was horrified during and after the movie. I couldn't waste any time; after all, torturing smaller children in the family is about as American as baseball and apple pie. So I waited. She was downstairs, being consoled by my mother, while I lay in wait. I was hiding under her bed. The only thing that could ruin my plan was my bad habit of not being able to conceal laughter. She finally came up the stairs and, after brushing her teeth, was about to enter another frightening experience. As the room got dark and she climbed into bed, I was biting holes through my tongue to avoid giving away my position with an unintended snicker. As I listened to her breathing, I knew I had to wait for that moment when I knew she had fallen asleep. The few minutes under that bed seemed to last for hours. Finally, I could tell she was out. I quietly slid my arm and hand between her mattress and the wall. I then proceeded to pin her body, with my arm, to the bed. It worked. She let out a scream that probably woke up every dog on West Center Street that night. Mission accomplished.

I then had to escape. I heard the distinctive sound of the recliner being lowered in the living room downstairs. He was coming. I quickly slid out from under my sister's bed and dashed across the hall to the room I shared with my brother. I was on the top bunk. No time to use the ladder. I jumped into bed, but in my haste, I kicked the long board that ran down the length of the bed. This board was supposed to keep children from slipping out of the top bunk. It never worked for me. I remember waking up on many a night when the back of my head hit the hardwood floor, which was about four feet down. The sound of the board rattling clued my belt-wielding father. The sting of his belt on my rear end was well worth it. The golden princess had been defeated, and at least for a day or two, I was my brother's hero.

The summertime in South Jersey was the best—baseball, the occasional Boy Scout camping trip, and more baseball! We never went on family vacations growing up. Instead, there was an occasional day trip to Hershey Park or a picnic somewhere in Maryland or Pennsylvania. If we weren't at the elementary school playing baseball, we were collecting baseball cards or coming up with new games that involved baseball.

Our backyard was tiny, but it was perfect for a game we developed called Puff Ball. A sidewalk leading from the back porch to the detached garage was the third baseline. A flagstone pathway, parallel to the garage, was the first baseline. A chain-link fence running from the garage to the house was the right field fence, center field was a garden of yew bushes and rhododendrons, and left field was the back porch. The dimensions were twenty feet down the lines and about thirty-five feet to dead center. Needless to say, even a Wiffle ball was out of the question. Our answer was a foam ball. You had to really hammer it to homer.

My brother and I both are left-handed hitters. With the breeze blowing in from right, it made it near impossible to homer in that direction. As a result, we both became very good at hitting the ball to the opposite field. The porch roof was now where most of the home runs landed. Years later, my high school baseball coach, in a rage, would ask, "Mr. Fields, why can't you pull the ball?" I decided the real answer would not have flown.

We were not satisfied with just playing our backyard games. I, of course, had to announce every play with my best Harry Kalas voice (the longtime Phillies broadcaster) and add fan noise as loud as possible. These actions were always met with the same result. "Boys, the windows are open. You are screaming at the top of your lungs!" I never quite figured out where the top of my lungs were. I guess that is one of those mysteries only a mother knows.

Back when I was growing up, ballplayers all chewed tobacco—not the sunflower seeds of today's players. You would see it on television, a big old lump sticking out of a player's cheek. Of course we wanted to emulate this, but there was no way we were going to try the real thing. That came later. Our answer was baseball cards. Back in my day, every pack of cards came with a stick of pink bubblegum. It was usually really hard and covered with a white powdery substance and tasted awful. If I recall, a pack of cards was fifteen cents, and in 1977, I actually collected the entire Topps set. The gum was set aside in an old cabinet my parents would put things in—flashlights, dog treats, you name it. When our pink cardboard tasting collection was big enough, it was time to get our chew on. We would stuff about twenty pieces in our cheeks, and we were big leaguers. With all those pieces of gum, the taste still faded in a matter of minutes. The result was that of tree bark or, at the least, cardboard. Didn't matter; it looked like chew.

Nothing made us happier than terrorizing our mother. Scaring her was an art form in our eyes. When she made her daily trip to the mailbox, one of us would always hide in the basement or some random room. When she entered the house, the moaning and faking of an injury would occur. She knew we were faking, but she would always wear down and come to investigate. That is when the other guy would jump out of a closet or from behind a chair and scare the crap out of her. There is something so funny about hearing your mother scream! However, embarrassing Mom is even greater. Many times in midafternoon, she would lie on the coach to rest her eyes for a few minutes. That is when the passing of gas started. My mother would let out little putters from her backside, and then it was on. One of us would ultimately wake her up and say, "Mom, you are farting in your sleep." She would deny that it happened. She denies it to this day. It is amazing that as middle-aged men, we would still ask her about it—but we are still little boys at heart. I could go on about my childhood forever, but I think you get the picture. Immaturity, passing gas, and screaming and being obnoxious for the sake of it was just the way we rolled in the '70s. After all, the television only had three channels, and video games consisted of riding your bike or seeing if a firecracker would blow up your model airplane.

HIGH SCHOOL

E VERYONE KNOWS WHAT high
school is about–gawkiness, dating for
the first time, planning for college or work–so I will not go into it. What I will
talk about is some of the funny things I experienced while playing high school
sports. My freshman basketball team struggled, to put it mildly. One win in
twenty games makes for a long season. I can recall an entire practice that
consisted of running suicides. Anyone who has ever played basketball knows
what they are. Suicides are not fun. These became a mainstay for my coach as
a form of punishment. One round of suicides in particular was deserved, but
well worth it.

The punishment occurred after a road game. The team bus was held up
for an hour or two. In pregame warm-ups, one of my teammates decided it
would be hilarious to "pants" another teammate in the layup line. To pants
someone, for those who don't know, is to come up behind them and yank their
shorts down to the ankles. This was the early '80s. Compression shorts were
not invented yet, so jockstraps were the weapon of choice for the male athlete.
When the act occurred, the victim decided to leave his game shorts at his ankles
and take his layup like he had been shackled. I can still see his bare-butted layup
being taken. There was nothing to hide it except for the straps on the back of his
jock. The team burst into laughter. The fans and, more importantly, our coach
were not amused. He never said a word.

After losing the game by forty points, we were instructed to stay on the
bench until the gym cleared out. I still think I have blisters on my feet from

that evening. Three years later, the same kid who had taken the bare-assed layup was at it again. It just so happened that my varsity baseball coach was also the freshman basketball coach. The good thing was, our baseball team was very good. Before games, the team would break up into groups. While the infielders were taking ground balls, the outfielders were taking fly balls. One of the nonstarters for that day's game would be responsible for hitting fly balls to the other outfielders. On this day, the layup-line legend had found out he was not starting the game. He proceeded to grab the box of brand-new game balls instead of the weathered brown practice baseballs that were normally used. He was smart about it–whenever he reached into the ball bag and found a new ball, he would proceed to hit that ball over the fence and into the creek that ran behind it. No one knew why he was hitting so many balls into the creek until the game was about to start. Our coach went into the dugout to grab the game-ball box, only to find that it was empty. That was when the rest of the team realized what had been taking place. The good news was that old baseballs can be used to play a game.

And then there were the bus rides! If you were not paying attention to your surroundings, a teammate would come up behind you and pin you to the seat. It was then time for the oxygen. Another player from the team would exclaim, "Someone needs air." That's when the protective cup was placed over the mouth and nose of the now-frantic player. Cup checks were also a constant reminder of the immaturity level of a high school ballplayer. A simple backhanded slap to the private parts of a teammate would usually attain the desired effect. Loud laughter, a groan, and sometimes the added bonus of having the young man fall to his knees.

I am sure that mooning was started about the time Henry Ford started rolling his Model T cars off the assembly line. I had a teammate who definitely took this sophomoric act to the next level. It was called *pressed ham*. Not only was the butt exposed to the passing car or unsuspecting pedestrian, the skin had to stick to the glass. To be accomplished without being caught by the coach, a human shield was usually set up by two or more of the boys. This blocked the view if, for some reason, the coach decided to turn around and survey the rear section of the bus. On this fateful day, the target was a carload of four older women. The trap was set, and the human shield was up. The pants then hit the floor. When the car passed the bus, the desired result occurred–four women with their mouths open, looking horrified. There was a major problem. They were all wearing funny-looking headwear. My teammate had mooned a carload of nuns. As a child who was raised Catholic, this disturbed me (though not enough to stop me from laughing), and I always stayed away from him during electrical storms from that day on.

I would be remiss if I didn't mention another story from my sports life in high school. It actually occurred during a week of basketball camp during the summer between my freshman and sophomore year. It was an outdoor camp, but during one rainy summer day, all the campers were forced inside for the day. As we entered the gym, we all noticed a very tall black man at the other end of the court. After one of the coaches went and talked to him, he approached us with some great news. The man was a backup center for the Philadelphia 76ers. He was working out in that gym during the off-season. After a brief coaching session by him and some questions and answers, he had a challenge for us. Remember, this man was at least six foot, eleven inches tall. If any of us could make a layup on him, he would present the camper with a brand-new one-hundred-dollar bill. All eighty or so of us lined up and tried to make a shot on this man. Not one of us succeeded in making a shot. I remember my attempt on him ended up about thirty rows in the stands. Then it happened. A smallish camper, I am guessing probably a fifth grader, took his turn. He dribbled straight at the man and gave him a head fake. For some reason, the NBA player left his feet to attempt a block. The little guy drove by him and hit a reverse layup. The place erupted! The player then waved his massive arms like a referee would when a pass was incomplete. "No reverse layups!" He shouted. We were stunned. The NBA player was then bum-rushed and hit with towels and gym bags. He walked out of that gym with a grin and a head shake. He never did give away the one hundred bucks.

DAD AND MOM

I TALKED ABOUT my father at the beginning of the book. He passed away from kidney cancer in 1993, just five years after he had retired from education and the meat-cutting world. He instilled in me the work ethic that made me into a decent employee for years, and he gave me the confidence to not be afraid of failure. He was very fond of saying, "Remember, that guy over there puts his pants on the same way–one leg at a time."

My mother loves to tell the story of their first date. It occurred at a movie theater. The movie was a full house, which tended to happen a lot back in the days before DVDs and home theaters. My dad was in the aisle seat next to my mother. Before the lights dimmed, he had decided to use the bathroom. This habit continued until the day he died. He knew where every rest stop and gas station restroom was in the whole northeastern section of the United States. After he returned to his aisle seat, he was immediately tapped on the shoulder. It was his date. He had mistakenly taken a seat in front of her that was empty. In my mother's telling, he turned around and surprisingly said, "What are you doing back there?" The lights had dimmed by this time, so when he attempted to return to his seat, he mistakenly sat down in the aisle. My mother's retelling of this story always brought her to tears of laughter, and to see my father's expression while she was telling it was priceless.

He was also one of the cheapest people I have ever known. He would spend hours clipping coupons for our weekly trip to the grocery store. This was back before the cashier was equipped with a scanner. Therefore, the process of entering all those coupons at checkout was long and embarrassing. You see, you had to find each item the coupon represented before getting credit for it. "R.A., can you find the toilet paper? I have a ten-cent coupon!"

If it was on sale, it was a deal. Even if it was a piece of clothing you really did not want. Kmart was the worst. Remember when that "blue light special" cart that used to light up in an area of the store? We had to rush over there like pigs to the slop to see what the deal was. I specifically remember a dress shirt he purchased for me for school. It was one color–the ugliest shade of brown I had ever seen. It was stiff as a board. It was like a piece of that pink gum with the white powder had morphed into a garment. It never got soft. I blame it for my chest hair only starting to grow in my midthirties. It was so rough; I used to wear a long-sleeved thermal shirt under it in September to keep from breaking out in a rash. Try wearing that to high school with a pair of brown corduroy pants. It is no wonder I didn't have a date in high school. If you asked for something for a birthday or Christmas, you would definitely get it. The thing was, it would be two years later, when the item had hit the discount rack!

He once called a family meeting to discuss the use of toilet paper in the house. All five children and my mother gathered in the living room. Not only were we using too much, we needed a lesson on how to properly use it. "This is how we all should be using the toilet paper," he stated as he slowly unrolled a tube. "You only need to use four of the squares, and after the first wipe, you can turn it over and get a second wipe." My older sisters were very embarrassed, but the younger siblings found it hilarious. He later took me aside with his theory on the overuse. He felt it was my oldest sister using it to wipe off her face after track practice. I told him he was probably correct. You see, I could play both sides of the fence also!

If you ever made the mistake of purchasing a record album, you had to try to avoid having him see you walk into the house with it. You see, my father had lived through the Great Depression, and albums to him were a waste of money. He would simply give you the stare and say, "You can't eat a record." My father wasn't much for eloquence, but he always made his point. Both my parents were very smart, and they could play you for a fool. I remember specifically asking for a gas-powered toy car when I was a ten-year-old. "Sure!" they said. "You can get it when you turn sixteen." Little did I know that sixteen-year-old-boys have other things on their mind.

My mother was very protective of my younger brother. After all, he had dark hair and brown eyes like his mom. She liked him so much, she even commented on the beauty of his brown eyes to my wife. It just so happened, it was on our wedding day! I am amazed I don't have even more issues at this point. I guess he didn't get enough attention from my mother, because as I soon found, the opposite sex in high school was not off-limits.

One day, I was approached by two female underclassmen that were not happy with me. They could not believe that I had locked my younger brother in the garage for a week and made him stay out there. My laughter to the accusation of the two girls only made them angrier. My response to them was, "Don't believe everything you hear." I did ask my brother, and he explained to me that he thought they had known he was only joking. I never bought into that. I really believed he loved their attention and the compassion he was receiving from them.

I, on the other hand, had the dirty-blond hair and the hazel eyes. My father used to tell me that my eye color was that of what an infant might leave in a diaper. I was a mixture of the blue-eyed blond father and the abovementioned mother. My mother would let my brother sleep in on school days, and he rarely got the look from her. The best way to describe that look is that it was a disgusted look only a mother could give.

I do recall, however, the day my brother almost died. To this day, the reason I think he pulled off this stunt was to make his older brother laugh. I am still laughing about it today. It was a late Sunday afternoon. My father was taking a nap in the recliner directly behind me, and I was on my belly, watching television. My brother came into the room and got my attention. As I looked up, he was pretending to read the TV Guide. I never understood why we needed one. It was not very hard to figure out what was on. He was leaning over the end table with his buttocks positioned about two inches from my father's chin and opened mouth. He then did the unthinkable. He unleashed from the back end. The sound can only be described as an untuned trombone. Within a millisecond, as I was barrel-rolling to safety, my father was out of the chair with a belt in hand. He caught my brother as he tried to escape to the kitchen and the safety of my mother. The whole first floor of the house was filled with my brother's screams and the sound of the leather belt against his rear end.

Of course, I was in tears too. The kind that stream from your eyes when you hear and see something that makes you come apart of yourself with laughter. My mother then came to the rescue. All I remember hearing was, "Dad, you're killing him!" My dad's response was not only direct but angry. "He farted in my face!" At this time, my brother was using the defense we had tried many times with mixed results. He was pretending to be unconscious. That defense, I will admit, never worked for me.

After the melee subsided, we retreated to our bedroom. With the door shut for several hours, my brother and I laughed and relived the moment, knowing full well that there would be more tears, belts, and laughter in our future. My brother used to say, "We are the only kids who get in trouble for laughing." He is correct, but the reason for it is the fact that we laughed every waking hour. My teachers, growing up, never saw this side of me. I was very respectful and quiet. When you have two parents at home whose college major was education, the last thing you wanted were bad reports sent home from school.

COLLEGE

A S YOU CAN see, I did survive the belt and growing up in southern New Jersey. It was now time to test the uncharted waters of higher education. I had decided a few years earlier to major in forestry. My first two years would be spent in a two-year college in Northwestern Pennsylvania. The third and fourth years were spent at a university located in Syracuse, New York. So on a hot August day in 1983, I loaded up the trunk of my father's Mercury Monarch and left my comfort zone to move into a dorm in La Plume, Pennsylvania.

My first roommate was a charming young man, to say the least. He spent most nights in the hallway, talking on the pay phone to his high school sweetheart back at home. He would spend hours telling her how much he loved her. The rest of his time at college was spent chasing every girl on campus. There were many nights I spent sleeping on a friend's floor so he could proclaim his love to that week's conquest. He was also forestry major. I guess that is why we were paired together as roommates. He rarely attended class and left school in the December of the first semester. I never heard from him again. My second roommate had a hobby, his body. He would spend hours working out in front of the mirror in our room with his shirt off. He once went an entire semester without saying a word to me. I guess you could say he was the strong, silent type. The last I heard of him was that he was one credit short from graduating with his associate's degree.

We did have a hobby on Monday nights—it was watching football in our room. My parents had given me an old black-and-white television to use in my dorm room. It came with rabbit ears and a volume control that sometimes worked. The only channel it got was the channel that happened to carry the weekly Monday night football game. We had to place the TV on a mountain of books just to get the reception right. That wasn't all, we had to remove the screens from our dorm room windows, and the windows had to be cranked out to their fully open position. The light from our dorm room allowed every moth in Pennsylvania to enter our room while we strained our necks to watch the game. I don't know why we just didn't walk down to the lounge to enjoy the game, but it seemed like fun at the time. After the game concluded each week, we opened our door and turned out all the lights, thus allowing all the night creatures to exit into the hallway. The swarm of insects exiting our room was a joy to behold.

Today's college student probably has zero idea of what we had to go through to enjoy a ball game in our room. My college baseball coach was probably the first person I had ever met that loved the game of baseball as much as I did. I used to love hearing him talk before and after practice. He was very fond of saying, "It will come out in the wash." That was his answer for a struggling player or a bad day of practice. It's a simple saying, but a saying that has stuck with me all these years.

My first day of practice was the day I realized that my major league dreams would soon be at an end. I was paired for stretching and throwing with the best baseball player I had ever seen. He could do everything well. He was a real five-tool player. Years later, he would retire at thirty-eight years old. He never made it to the show. The triple-A level was his limit. Years later, when I had the opportunity to coach high school baseball, I would bring him up as an example of how good you really had to be to have a chance at the big leagues.

During my high school days, I had started a habit that I did not break for a long time–running. I figured if I was not the best athlete, I could be in better shape than anyone else. In late October of my first semester, an event took place that put my running to use. During Parents Weekend, there would be a five-mile cross-country race through the woods and trails behind campus. I signed up. After all, I would run five miles every morning. My dad called me early that week to let me know he would be driving up for the weekend. This would be the only time in my college career that a parent would visit me, so I was going to make him proud. The event was to take place at 8:00 a.m. on Saturday morning. It would be followed by the women's and men's soccer games. The race would begin and end in the soccer stadium. Twenty runners would start by running two laps around the stadium before the cross-country part of the race began. I was excited, and I wanted to win the prize for finishing first–a billy goat! I figured at least that would be a roommate who would talk to me.

The starter pistol was fired, and we were off. My adrenaline must have been overflowing because I started the way I had hoped to finish. I was sprinting around that stadium and had a very sizable lead entering the trails. My race was over. At about the two-mile mark, I began to hear footsteps. It was the sound of runners catching up. One by one, they passed, and there was nothing I could do. As I approached the soccer stadium, I was in about tenth place. As another runner approached and passed me, I noticed as he went by, he had a cast on his arm. I realize at that point, I was not taking home a goat, but there was no way in hell a guy with a broken arm was going to beat me. I did have a little pride. As I entered the stadium, I could see the first group finishing. I had my eyes set on that plaster-covered arm. I had a little left in the tank, so I used it to catch him and finish the race in tenth place. I had caught and beaten the one-armed man!

I found out later that the goat was a prop and was returned to the farmer that had loaned the college the animal for the event. I can tell you now that I would not have given that goat back, not without a fight. I was and still am an animal lover and have never met one that I am not fond of.

My father and I enjoyed a nice day together. We took in a movie (no, he didn't fall in the aisle) and gorged on pizza. It was the best weekend I ever had at college.

One of the things I took away from Boy Scouts was to always be prepared. This also came into play while I navigated my way through a college course load. There is always an exception. In order to transfer all my credits to the university I was to transfer to in 1985, there were certain courses that I had to take without exception. One of these happened to be Public Speaking 101. This is probably the class I dreaded most of all. People who know me now confuse my stand-up–comedian persona to an absence of shyness. This has never been the case. I am painfully shy; but once I get to know you, I have no problems acting extroverted. Another way I cover for being shy is to act the part of a stand-up comedian when in mixed company.

Well, I waited until my sophomore year to take this course. Finally, the time came for my first of ten speeches I was to be graded on that semester. I did my due diligence. I prepared, made sure the speech was well written, and made sure all the facts were in order. I bombed! The professor said I had not prepared, and my first speech had received a big fat D. That is when I decided to experiment. I was going to go into the next speech and totally wing it. It worked; I came up with a topic about five minutes before it was my turn and let her rip! The teacher was impressed with the improvement. I received a B. He went on to say, "See what happens when you do a better job preparing?" I simply nodded my head in approval and went on to perform my stand-up act eight more times. No notes, no getting facts straight; I just picked up a subject to talk about that day then stood up and talked about it. I guess I had the ability to act confident even if I wasn't. My grades didn't drop off from the B average I had carried throughout high school.

The small campus and not having distractions of following division 1 sport programs had made the transition easier than I had hoped. That would sure change in 1995, as I made the trek to Syracuse, New York, and experienced some of the coldest weather I could ever imagine. The forestry school in Syracuse is a school within a school. It is a state school within the confines of the large university. Compared to the schools I had come from, it was easy to get lost in the large campus community. It also came with more distractions.

Of course, my first night on campus, I proved that only I could make the campus small. My roommate, a guy I had become friends with during my first two years, had talked me into exploring the campus nightlife. He didn't have to try very hard. We picked a local watering hole just off campus and began to indulge. I had noticed a pretty blond coed sitting alone. I did say earlier that I was shy, but beer seemed to make that a moot point. I introduced myself and spent about three hours making a complete ass out of myself. My first day of class was the following morning. As I was sitting at my desk, I felt a tap on the shoulder and heard the words "good morning, R.A." It was her, the girl from the night before. In a campus of over twenty thousand students, only I could have met the one destined to be seated next to me!

After that embarrassing moment, my next order of business was to purchase season tickets for the two major sports. Football tickets were easy to come by. It was a different story for basketball season tickets. They were ordered in a lottery system. You had to stand in line on several separate nights outside of the domed stadium just to get your number. I believe, if memory serves me correctly, it took five visits to the dome to finally purchase season tickets for that year. If it wasn't team sports that kept me from hitting the books, it was the activities on and off campus. There was always something going on, and I was a willing participant. The grades I had achieved in high school and junior college were a thing of the past, and I was on academic probation for three of the five semesters it took me to acquire my bachelor's degree. My college career ended at the end of December in 1987, and I was relieved and happy it did. I never could understand why a career planned on working outdoors was mainly taught inside. I spent many a class staring out those windows, wishing I was there.

It was time for my work career to begin. I had a taste of it during my tenure of higher education. After my freshman year in college, I had gotten a job working at a local gas station in my hometown. It was within bike-riding distance from home, so not having a car did not come into play. I worked for a family-run business that was owned by two brothers, who had inherited the business from their father. Pumping gas, changing oil, fixing flats, and cleaning the garage were my main duties. Each brother would have the responsibility of opening the shop every other week because there was no way they were going to let a college kid have keys to do so. I was always the first one there at 7:00 a.m. Most of the time, one of them would roll in at 7:00 a.m. or a few minutes after. I did say most of the time. I would be patiently waiting with my trusty bicycle, ready to make that minimum wage.

Then one fateful morning, it happened–no one showed. I had one option: I could ride my bike the three miles to his house and wake him up. The whole ride over, I kept thinking he probably passed me on his way in, and he was going to accuse me of being late. I made it to the co-owners' house and could see that his '70s-style conversion van was still in the driveway. I knocked on the front door for about ten minutes. Nothing! My next move was to start up his push lawn mower and let it run underneath his bedroom window. After about ten minutes of this, I saw his pillow-headed face behind the screen. He then asked, "What the hell is you doing?" When I told him it was eight o'clock, he told me to take his keys and open up. I rode my bike back and opened the garage. I no sooner got the key in the door when he pulled up in his van. I still do not know why I couldn't have put my bike in the van and driven in with him.

The nice thing about the job was that they liked having me around, and it gave me some extra money over Christmas and spring breaks for the rest of my college career. Then the offer came in. They sat me down one day before I was to return to campus and wanted to talk. "Would you consider being our full-time apprentice and learn the trade?" My question to them was what the pay would be. The response was minimum wage. I did not take them up on their offer. My life would have been much different than it is today. After all, these were the two guys who would be in the front office, enjoying coffee and reading the morning paper when the bell would ring, meaning we had a gas customer. "You got one up" is what I'd hear. Never mind that I was underneath a lift, covered in oil. It was my job to pump the gas. They avoided that at all costs, and furthermore, they would rag on me for making the customer wait. I always threatened to not clean the oil off my hands the next time it happened, but I never went through with it. I guess I understood about good customer service at a young age.

My last three summers during my college career were spent in the Adirondack Mountains of New York state. It was not the way most college kids spent their summer vacations. I would be attached to a chainsaw and the wonderful world of the lumberjack. It was bruising work, to say the least. Pulpwood was the order of the day. We were to supply the paper companies the wood they needed to make writing paper, etc. Four college kids would work alongside the permanent crew in the summer months. During the rest of the year, local inmates would be the crew of choice. The nice thing about the job was a free room. It was an A-frame in the middle of a pristine forest campus the college owned in the northeastern part of the state. My parents would drop me of in the middle of May and pick me up at the end of August to return to campus. My vacation would start then when I returned to campus, and as I said, my grades reflected that.

The first two weeks were always spent working for the National Forest Service. The plan was simple enough. Each student was to plant about one thousand seedlings a day. The job involved carrying the seedlings in a bag and, with a long shovellike tool, planting them in areas that had been clear-cut in the past. There were two major problems: (1) the clear-cut areas were overgrown with raspberry plants that were loaded with thorns and (2) May in the Adirondacks is blackfly season. This made for a lovely first two weeks of summer vacation. You simply would walk out into the clear-cut and, in a straight line, dig a slit into the earth and plant a tree. Ten feet later, you would repeat the process until your bag was gone. The raspberries in these clear-cuts were ten feet high, and the thorns would rip into you and draw blood. Long sleeves, hard hats, and long pants were mandatory; but this did not stop your skin from being ravaged. Swarms of blackflies would follow you everywhere, and it was mentally exhausting as well as physically. You could not see the other workers in the field due to the vegetation, but you could definitely hear the cursing and skin being slapped. I distinctly remember a fellow worker screaming out, "I can't take these f—king bugs anymore!" It was the sound of a young man being broken, but it made for great comic relief, as far as I was concerned. I spent the next minute on my back, laughing.

Even with all the protective clothing, I felt like one big welt when it was quitting time. After two weeks of this, I couldn't wait to get my hands on a chainsaw. The bluish smoke they emit is, in my opinion, the best blackfly repellent known to man. Although most of the summer was spent felling trees and bucking them up to pulpwood-sized lengths, a need to do another task would sometimes arise. One of these jobs occurred because of a family of beavers. They had dammed up a small pond and flooded one of the many forest roads. Our job was to break down their home and let the water recede to its original spot. The job was given to me and one of the full-time employees. He was an old-timer and a very hardworking man. To be honest, he was not the brightest of men; but if you needed something done, he would do it, no questions asked. We parked and waded out into the water. The beavers had seen us and they got out of there and did what angry beavers do. They began to slap the water with those big canoe oar-looking tails. As we tore down their home, the old-timer asked me, "R.A., who is throwing rocks at us?" For a second, I was dumbfounded. Then I realized the sound of the slapping water he was mistaking for rocks landing in the pond. I turned and told him it wasn't rocks; it was the beavers. His response was classic. "Why are they throwing rocks at us?" Some questions you just can't answer.

As I stated before, I did not own a car. My first car was actually not purchased until I had graduated college. The closest town from our forest was about seven miles away. It had one stoplight, two bars, a grocery store, and a Laundromat. Once a week, I would make the trek down to stock up on groceries and launder my clothes. If none of the other students were around on weekends, I would make the trip on that trusty ten-speed. It was great going into town. Going straight down the mountain, I barely had to pedal. The trip back was a lot more challenging with a duffel bag loaded with clean clothes and some groceries on the handle bars. It is a wonder I survived to tell this tale. Logging trucks would blow by on your trip, blowing their horns as they passed. I am sure it was an attempt to scare me. The force of the passing truck would almost suck you under. All that work for some hot dogs and clean underwear!

The three years working there provided memories and experiences I will never forget. Somehow, I survived fighting a forest fire, having large trees dropped in my general direction, and most of all, all the bugs. I used to often wonder during those summers, Was any other college student working this hard?

WORK LIFE

AS I STATED earlier, I added an extra semester at Syracuse and graduated in December of 1987. It was just the way I liked it. No fanfare, just simply having my college career over with. Before I left campus, I had visited the job board at the counseling office and copied down some information on job openings. Now it was back to my home in New Jersey.

It didn't take long for the phone to ring, and I jumped at the chance to join the workforce and be out on my own. A company in Michigan had called, and they were looking for a forester to work with the power company in that state. The call came on a Thursday; the job started the next Monday. That night, my father helped me purchase my first set of wheels–a pickup truck; and I left for the state of Michigan early on Saturday morning. I would drive up to western New York that day, spend the night at my college girlfriend's house, then drive to Michigan, via Canada, on Sunday. I had received another phone call before I left from a fellow graduate who was also starting the same job as I. That would make the transition easier and give me a roommate when I got settled in. I enjoyed the new job and my new nickname. I was called "Jersey" by the other employees when I checked in once a week at the office. The rest of the week was spent making sure the power lines were free of tree limbs. My job was to get property owner's okay for any removals I deemed necessary. Since the power company owned the right of way, there was no need to get permission for removals. As long as my paperwork was in order and I could keep three tree crews busy, there were not any problems.

The problem was in the apartment. My roommate was just one of those guys. We all know them, a twenty-one-year-old who has all the answers. He was an expert on everything. Music, women, and world politics were just some of the things he felt he was an authority on. I will give him credit for one thing. He was an authority on smoking pot and not going to work. Remember, you only had to check in to the office once a week. That was the only day of the week he was actually out the door with me in the morning. I still don't know how he faked the numbers. My theory was, he had enough built up to keep the crews busy, but his luck would run out soon enough. It never came to that. It was contract work.

I was actually working for another company that was contracted out by the power company. Late that summer, one of my bosses told me that the company was looking to cut us loose. They felt that the work could be done cheaper by keeping the work in house. It was very nice of him to give me the heads-up, and I began my search for employment elsewhere.

Whatever happened to the pot smoking roommate, you ask? He, of course, landed on his feet. I ran into him several years ago. He has a job with the state, still is an expert on everything, and still treats marijuana like I treat air.

I left Michigan in the fall of 1988 and moved to what would be my home base for seventeen years, Western New York. Yes, I moved to my college sweetheart's hometown. She had given me a lead on a job with a tree company. It was my introduction to the world of pesticides, bad bosses, and health issues. If I had the ability to look into a crystal ball at this point in my life, I probably wouldn't have believed it. In a few short years, the college sweetheart would be out of my life, and I would begin the odyssey that brings me to this point in my life.

I packed that pickup truck with my belongings, and once again, I took the long drive through Canada to the United States border at Niagara Falls. I started a new job with a tree and lawn-care company. Things went well for two years. The problem with this job was the dreaded winter layoff. That is where I hooked up with a small-business owner. My winters were spent roofing or doing the occasional siding job. Times were tough, but my bosses were great at this time, and I was really enjoying life. Winters in Western New York are brutal. This does not make roofing the job of choice for anyone. However, working under the table and keeping up on my bills kept me going through the punishment my body was taking at the time.

There was always a chance for comic relief. One of these times occurred during a fall I took during a large reroofing job. The house was huge and ancient. It had been reroofed at least four times, and it was our job to tear the existing shingles off to expose the plywood underneath. The problem was that years of water and ice damage had begun to rot the wood underneath. My boss kept telling me to be careful where I stepped. "It is rotten underneath," he kept exclaiming. Sure enough, I misstepped and fell through into an upstairs bedroom. My legs were dangling just above a child's bed. My boss was not happy. He kept saying, "I told you to be careful. Now we're going to have to fix the ceiling." I understood his anger. Being a small-business owner, I can only imagine how one feels when extra costs are incurred.

About an hour after my mishap, the comedy act was just getting started. My boss fell through. I mean he went all the way in! When I went through the roof, my legs went in, but I pulled myself back to the safety of the outside. He was not so lucky. He fell through all the way and landed on the kitchen table. The problem was, the homeowner was sitting at that table, enjoying his morning coffee and reading a newspaper. I will never forget his reaction. You have to remember that he was covered with old shingles and dust. He simply looked up from his newspaper and politely asked, "Would you like a cup?" I was looking through the huge hole that had been created by the mishap and could not help but laugh. My addition to the commotion was to state the obvious to my now embarrassed but laughing boss. "I thought you told me to be careful" was the sarcastic comment I used to lighten the mood even more.

My boss had a great sense of humor and was a great person to work for. I really enjoyed my times roofing, except for the punishment my body was taking. I hope, for his sake, that he is in a different line of work now. He was a thirty-five-year-old man then, with the body of a sixty-year-old. Besides, this was just a pit stop on my road to becoming a park ranger. If only I knew what was in store for me.

At this time, my summers were spent spraying trees for pests and disease. I was the clean-cut college boy at the company, so I was given a route that placed me in the well-off suburban section of town. I got my first taste of how snobby people can really be. I was called "boy" on a regular basis and talked down to every day. It was hard biting my tongue, but I made it through. This was my first experience with customer service, but it wouldn't be the last. Biting my tongue would become a lot harder to do, and I would fail at that more than I would succeed.

Being laid off during the winter months was the main reason I started the next phase of my life. It would involve being a customer service representative for a lawn-care company. My tree-spraying days were over, and so was the string of good bosses. I landed the job mainly due to my education and the fact that I had attained a pesticide applicator license at my old job. Anyone who has ever done lawn care for a living knows how hard it really is. You basically are a company owner within a company. The problem is, you are not just the owner. You are the grunt who takes care of all the lawns. This involves pushing a rotary spreader for eight to ten hours every day during the spring, summer, and fall. You are also the salesman for your company. This is done in the winter months and in the summer evenings after you have been physically drained by the demands of the job.

Dealing with customer complaints on a daily basis is another part of the job. You see a lot of the people who sign up for lawn care are misinformed. For some reason, they think that if their lawn is treated four or five times a year, they will have a property that will rival a fairway at Augusta. Somehow, they never understood that watering, proper mowing, overseeding, and aeration were also factors that played into having that lush green lawn they were looking for. It was frustrating and very hard work. You could be cruising along one minute and have a thunderstorm pop up out of nowhere. Sure, the fertilizer was being watered in, but also, all those weeds you had just treated were in the back of your mind. Heavy rain tends to wash liquid spray off weed leaves, causing you not to get very good weed control.

Management in this company didn't care that you had to go back and retreat a lawn for free. The bottom line was the most important thing to them. If you didn't bill a certain amount a day, you were coming in on the weekend or you were being replaced. Quality of work had little bearing on how they valued you as an employee. You had to hit your numbers in sales and the amount of work you billed on a daily basis to stay on the good side of management.

If you are looking to lose weight, this is a great job for you. The spreader you push can hold up to eighty pounds of fertilizer, and back in those days, you were the motor. I see today that workers can actually ride their spreader around the lawn they are treating. My day started at seven o'clock in the morning, and by ten, my bagged lunch was already history. Some days, I would stop two more times to refuel my body. It was easy for me to lose fifty pounds during the summer months.

Most of the guys I worked with were great guys, and we did have a lot of laughs. I remember this one guy who pulled into work on his first day in an old, broken-down Volvo. He was so broke he didn't have a key for it. He had just jammed an old butter knife in the ignition. He figured that no one was going to steal this old bucket of bolts anyway. We were all assigned two-way radios so we were always available to be reached by the office. It was really the only entertaining thing during most of those long summer days when you were out servicing lawns. This one particular time, I was in a backyard and found an old butter knife. I could not resist. I called my now friend on the radio and asked if he wanted me to get it for him. He could use it as a spare key for his car. No one was off-limits to being insulted on the radio.

There were always guys who would try to beat the system, and they were usually easy to spot. You just know they were cutting corners by the way they acted and how early they would be back at the shop after the workday. We had a few who would not even service lawns. They would just put the little flags on the property (the flags would tell the time and date of the application), and they would put the bill on the customer's door. They couldn't get away with it for long. Thirty calls from angry customers stating that their lawn was never done tend to raise red flags. I often wondered how long some of these guys got away with it before they were actually caught. Inevitably, they were caught and asked to leave the company immediately.

The term we coined for not really doing the lawn was "ghosting." It was open season on the radio when you got your chance to rag on a fellow employee. If someone would make the mistake of letting the rest of the guys know they were heading back to the shop a little early, the radio would light up with shouts of "Casper" or "ghost." Anything to berate a fellow worker seemed to make the day go a little smoother. As I remember, I was constantly being reminded by management to only use the radio for work-related issues. It never stopped me. It was just too much fun.

The longer I worked for this company, the worse it got. With most of the jobs I have worked in, we were assigned uniforms. On this one particular day, we all noticed that one of the other workers had returned to the shop in his street clothes. Alongside him on the seat of his truck was a garbage bag. Apparently, as he fertilized a steep hill in some customer's backyard, he had slipped and rolled entirely down the hill. The reason he had returned to the shop in his regular clothes was the substance that covered the hill. It so happened that the customer had used that hill to deposit the entire dog poop that built up in his yard. The worker was covered head to toe in dog feces, and you could smell him and his truck as he approached the shop. Of course, to a man, not one of us felt sorry for him. It was just the way we were. We were just looking for another thing to bust his chops about. New management, as I stated before, was interested in one thing—the bottom line. And he was forced to work the weekend to make up for his bad day.

About five years into my career at this company, we were purchased by a larger company. It was great news for me. I really wanted a change and wanted to get away from the use of pesticides on a daily basis. So in the spring of 1997, I was a free agent once again. It was now time to stop being covered with pesticides. They would be replaced with bodily fluids and athletic field paint. At this time, I was still trying to gain employment with a park service, but it seemed futile. I always was turned away, and that dream died somewhere in the late nineties.

Fortunately, during my time at the lawn-care company, I met my future wife. Of course, we had met on a blind date. With my work schedule at the time, it was nearly impossible for me to summon up the energy to hit the dating scene. We were hitched in the summer of 1996 and are still together to this day. I am sure she could add a lot to this book!

My next stop was working for a large cemetery, and I can honestly say this was the worst job I have held to this date. Not only was the job as depressing as you can imagine. For the most part, the people I worked with did not make the job of dealing with death any easier. I was on the internment crew. Yes, we were the crew who put your loved ones in their final resting place. It was a large cemetery, so funerals went on year-round. The two skills I learned from working here were operating a backhoe with precision and becoming numb to death. It just became part of the job. I would be lowering a casket into its vault, and I could hear the family sobbing and crying out. It was probably their worst day on earth, but I was simply doing a job and could not afford to mourn with them. You quickly learn that morbid humor is your only defense against becoming more depressed than the job already makes you.

Many of the guys on the crew were holdovers from the '70s and had been employed there for over twenty years. They were very hard to get along with and very paranoid. Each one of these guys had a vice and was more concerned with the fact that they had seniority than doing the job correctly. They had theories on everything. One guy even thought I was an undercover police officer looking to break up a drug ring at the park. Of all the jobs I have had in my career, it was the worst by far.

Since I was the new guy and the one with a college education, I was assigned most of the worst jobs that came along. Any disinterment was assigned to me as soon as it came along. Let it be noted that I was not the guy operating the backhoe; I was the guy down in the hole with the remains. When you are disinterring a body, there are factors involved in the job to take into consideration. First of all, you have to suit up. That means head to toe, full rubber suit with goggles, boots, and gloves. It doesn't matter if it is ninety degrees out; you have to protect yourself from blood-borne pathogens. This also means that your shots have to be up-to-date.

The hole is made to the side of the body, provided there is not another person buried next to the person you are removing. Once the hole is created, you are the person who is going down into the hole to guide the removal process. Most of the time, the old vault has filled with water, and this tends to speed up the rotting process of the human body. If by chance, the vault has been broken from years of being underground or being nicked by a backhoe, it tends to erupt with a gush of water when exposed to the elements. This is when it hits you. The god-awful smell! There are no words I can tell you to describe this aroma. If you have ever smelled it, you know what I mean. It is a smell that you will never forget, and it stays with you, days after the job is completed.

If you get lucky, the casket is still intact. If it was a metal casket, you have luck on your side, and you can move the remains to their new resting spot in an easier manner. It seems like during most of my time spent doing this horrible work, the caskets were always made of wood. Wood, as you might expect, does not hold up too well underground. If I was lucky enough, I was only dealing with skeletal remains; most of the time, I was dealing with rotten flesh.

Hollywood cannot come to close to describing the metamorphosis a human body goes through when it returns to the earth. I would commonly pretend I was dealing with alien remains to get through the process of moving the human remains to a new casket. The body, if you are wondering, could rarely be transferred to the new casket in one piece. Yes, I began to look for a new employer shortly after my start at the cemetery.

I would spend about two years there, but there were some entertaining moments. One occurred when a widow had found out that her late husband wasn't the most faithful person when he was alive. She would arrive at the park early every day. She would park near her husband's grave and march directly over to it. Then she would hike up her skirt and give him his daily shower. Yes, you read that correctly. She would urinate on his marker stone. Whoever coined the phrase "Hell hath no fury like a woman scorned" was right on the money.

Another memory of the job involved my attempt at giving a gift. If you have ever attended a funeral service, you know that they tend to be decorated with a large amount of flowers. Now, I have never been the most romantic guy, and my wife would attest to that, but I have attempted at times to do nice things for my wife. This time, I can only describe as an epic failure. My idea was simple. Why let these beautiful flowers go to waste? I picked out a beautiful bouquet and brought it home. I set it on the kitchen table so she could see it when she walked in the door. "Are those grave flowers?" she asked as soon as she walked in. "That is gross!" My plan had failed, and the worst part of it, I had forgotten to take the ribbon off the arrangement that said, "Mother." My wife and I still laugh about it today.

One of my fellow workers was prone to stuttering. The beauty of it was that he only stuttered when he was lying. This came in quite handy at times. He would be spinning one of his many tall tales, and his upper lip would start quivering, and you would know he was embellishing the story. We had an answering machine in the office that would record messages when employees would call in sick for the workday. Oftentimes, my boss would leave the door open, and all the guys could hear the recorded messages. On this particular day, the employee with the stammer was calling in. My boss pushed the button, and we heard a clicking sound and a person hanging up. This continued three or four times before we realized what was happening. He was not sick, but he was trying to say he was. He couldn't get through the lie and was struggling to get the words out. The crew went ballistic, to the ire of my boss. He slammed the door shut and told us to clear out. I never found out if he could get the words out to leave a complete message.

My prayers were finally answered, and after two years of trying, I began a four-year stint as a groundskeeper at a nursing home. The nursing home was a good place to work. There were a lot of dedicated employees and, like other stops along the way, people who just collected a paycheck. The grounds were beautiful, and I was responsible for keeping them that way. It truly was a labor of love. The problem was, I was the only person employed there to see that the grounds stayed that way. I was spread very thin, but I found a way to make it work. As in working for any nonprofit organization, the budget was tight. Yearly raises were always a crapshoot, and getting supplies needed for the job was interesting, to say the least. The residents were very appreciative of the gardens and grounds, so I would say that it was a success. After all, they were the people who we were trying to please and make happy.

From early November to late April, I was on call twenty-four hours a day, seven days a week. The reason for this was keeping the sidewalks and parking lot clear of snow and ice. There was no backup plan in place. I was the only one responsible for this. The small maintenance staff could not be bothered with it. Yes, to say a lot of the staff was lazy would be an understatement.

I shared my office/shop with a grounds manager at an adjoining apartment complex for seniors. He was managed by the same company who managed the nursing home. His theory on life was to be nice to everyone. It definitely wasn't working at his trade. He would do anything possible to get out of working. When one of us would go on vacation, the other would cover his workload for the week. The first week I ever covered for him, I mowed the complex in one day. Little did I know that he used to stretch out the task for three days. He figured if the residents saw him on the mower, they would not bother him with service calls in their apartments. When he came back from his vacation, he was furious with me. How could I make him look bad and do a three-day job in one? This is the same guy who used to come back an hour early for lunch so he could wash the lawnmower off, only to ride out on it again after his lunch break was over. He also took whining to a level I had never seen reached. It was always too cold or too hot for him. I often asked him why he chose this profession if he didn't like the elements. It definitely wasn't because he was talented at it. I often wonder why so many of the people I have worked with have this same attitude toward the job. I'm sure they could have found more suitable employment in a more-comfortable environment.

He was not lazy, however, when it came to playing practical jokes. You had to constantly check your surroundings when you entered our shop. Your chair would be attached to the wall or the seat on your mower would be greased.

My response to one of his jokes was both childish and amusing, as far as I was concerned. The night after I had slid off my mower I spent making a large supply of confetti with a hole punch. When I had enough to make my statement, I bagged the collection and waited for the next day. I normally arrived at the job before him, so there was ample time to put my plan to work. I took handfuls of the homemade confetti and placed it inside the dashboard vents inside his work truck. I then set his blowers on high speed then sat and waited for my prey. He jumped in his truck and started the engine. At that moment, the vents threw the small paper holes everywhere in his truck. For a split second, it looked like a full-sized snow globe had come to life! It was beautiful to see.

As I stated before, working for a nonprofit business has its shortcomings. Getting overtime pay was one of them. Although I removed snow for many hours during the winter months, my paycheck never seemed to increase. I was cut off for the day's work when I hit the eight-hour mark. Weekends were different. I could get some overtime in my paycheck, but management would try to not call me in on weekends unless it was absolutely necessary. I can understand the quandary they were in, but it did make doing the job more difficult. Of course, exceptions to the rules always exist. Nonprofit doesn't exactly mean what I thought it did. Someone sure made a profit, and by looking at the vehicles driven by upper management, I realized where it was being funneled.

I will talk more about bosses in a later section, but I wanted to relate an amusing story about this chapter of my working life. There was a change made at the nursing home. During my tenure there, the director of buildings and grounds had been removed. He had been there over fifteen years, and to put it mildly, it was time for him to pursue another career. The search was on for his replacement, and a lot of qualified candidates had been interviewed. When the choice was made, it shocked everyone employed there. His replacement was an employee who had worked at the nursing home for years in the housekeeping department. Yes, she was a dedicated and good employee, but she had no business running the department. She had no experience with maintenance or, for that matter, the maintenance of grounds. To say she was in over her head was an understatement.

She didn't like independent workers. So I was off to a rough start. She would often relay to me that no one knew what I did all day. My response would always be "All they have to do is look outside." This wasn't the answer she was looking for, so I was given the added responsibility of completing a daily logbook. This would give her the insight she would need to better manage me. On her first day as my manager, she told me that the only thing she would ever have a problem with was the clashing of colors in a flower garden. She told me to never to plant a red flower next to a pink one because she would have a real problem with that. I am sure there was a smirk on my face after hearing this was not very much appreciated, but I took that statement and kept it in my back pocket for a later date. On my last day employed at the nursing home, I replied to that request as only a groundskeeper could. I purchased a packet of pink tulip bulbs and a packet of red ones. The next spring, the garden next to the employee entrance was a clash of colors. I got great satisfaction knowing she walked by this garden on her way in to work every day!

My next stop would be my longest. I accepted a job with a school district, and for the next ten years, I would again battle lazy coworkers, open-heart surgery, and my return to baseball. (As a coach) I would enjoy some of the funniest moments in my life, as well as look death in the eye. My job title would be "maintenance mechanic," but this was only a title. I was still a groundskeeper, and 90 percent of my days were spent on playing fields and in gardens. The other portion of my job would find me behind the wheel of a plow truck, keeping the district clear of the snowfall that sometimes seemed to last from October to May during the harshest years.

I knew from day one that I had my work cut out for me. The school district had plenty of gardens, but their idea of an ornamental plant was a yew bush with an oak tree growing through it. It was my first initiation with a union job, and some of the old-timers took full advantage of the union's protection. You had to take your break at the same time every day. The problem with this was that they wanted you to take the break in the same place. You could be working at another building several miles away, and they would want you to drive back to the shop fifteen minutes early so you were on time for your break. To say the least, the beginning of my tenure at the school district was frustrating.

A lot of the teachers also had an attitude when it came to dealing with me. In my first two years at this job, one of my goals was to get the gardens in front of each building looking presentable. This particular day, I was in front of the middle school, planting some perennials in front of the large sign. A teacher walked up to me and asked, "Do you even know what you are planting?" I looked up to see the smug look on her face. I couldn't resist the temptation, and in a sarcastic voice, I responded with the Latin name of the particular plant I was working with. The building maintenance staff was just as bad. They would comment on what I was doing constantly. Things like "I don't know why you are planting things there." And they would say, "Nothing will ever grow there." My response would be "Just wait and see." A few years later, my harshest critic would actually apologize to me about how he had treated me as a new employee. He said I had proved him wrong and that the district had never looked better.

The beauty of working here was that I had free rein. My supervisor never cared about what I was doing, and I created several attractive flower beds with cuttings from my own beds at home. The problems arose because of something called chain of command. You see, people started noticing the person who was actually doing the work and began to know my name. Your superiors tend not to like someone who is below them on the totem pole getting credit for the things that are being accomplished on their watch. Administrators–who had never even seen my boss–just assumed I was the head groundskeeper. It was never my intent to undercut my boss, but when you work with someone who would rather be in his office on the computer or talking with other employees, these things tend to happen. The coaching staff would also treat me like I was in charge. This tends to happen when you are the person seen working on their playing fields.

One day, I had the vice principal come up to me after a fire drill. Apparently, one of the children had walked through the fresh topsoil and seed we had put down to fix the past winter's plow damage. She called me over and wanted me to know what the student could do to make up for the damage he had caused. That was when I introduced her to my boss, to see what he would like to be done. Her reaction later on was priceless. "Who was that?" she asked the building secretary. "I have never seen him before. I thought R.A. was the head groundskeeper." The problem with that was my boss had been employed at the district for ten years.

It is a funny thing that a lot of the administrators, teachers, and coaches think they could do the job of a groundskeeper and have no problem telling you so. I am sure if I ever showed up in one of their classrooms and critiqued the job they did, they would probably have a different reaction than I did. This is not to say that I always kept my mouth shut. My wife calls this my Jersey side. East Coasters tend to be more in-your-face and direct than most of the other parts of the country, and over the years, I have offended more than my share of people with my directness. I never understood when asked a question, the answer had to be sugarcoated. If you don't want an answer to your question, why ask it? My father never sugarcoated anything, and I think I turned out okay.

The things I heard teachers say would sometimes be shocking. If any educators are reading this book, here is a hint. Be careful what you say when you are walking across a campus. There may be a person lurking in the bushes. Of course, I was in there pruning or weeding, not lurking there, waiting to pass out candy. I often heard teachers talking about how they couldn't wait for summer vacation. Now don't take this the wrong way; teachers work hard. After all, both my parents were in the profession, but they seem to let you know how hard they work all the time. With the oncoming of social media, the things I read about teachers are all about self-promotion. They get the summers off, more holidays than the average worker, and in a lot of cases, are protected with tenure. It's something a person in my line of work will never get. Would

I want to do their job? No, but I could rattle off plenty of jobs that are more demanding and do not get the attention that they do. After all, not every fireman is a hero, not every lawyer is a money grubber, and not every teacher went into the profession to mold the youth of America.

This leads me to the epic battle I had with a teacher at this stop in my life. She was a teacher in the middle school. My office was also located here, and I often saw the teachers entering the building on their way in for work. She had a beautiful chocolate Labrador retriever that she would bring to school every day. She was a pet therapy dog. She would wander the halls during the day, spreading goodwill to the students and help them get through their day. She would also leave a gift to me outside the teacher's entrance every day. Now if you do this line of work, you know that you will come across your fair share of doggy droppings. It just comes with the territory. I just couldn't believe a teacher would have the nerve to let her dog do its business at the entrance of the school she worked and not have the courtesy to clean up after it. After witnessing this, I called the school principal to ask her if I was responsible for cleaning up after the pet therapy dog in her school. The answer was a resounding no. She was to clean it up. I had offered, and I thought this would be the end of it.

Boy was I wrong. The next three mornings, the dog did her business in the same spot, and the meadow muffins were beginning to pile up. I then took it upon myself to mail this teacher a couple of bags in our inner-school mail system. This was not received well. I received a nasty email from her. She stated in her letter that I was harassing her and that she had been having her students pick up the poop. Imagine that? Sending your students out to clean up the mess you were too lazy to pick up yourself. I knew what she was doing. She wanted a response from me so she could prove to the superintendent that I was the one who was harassing her and sending the bags. I gave her what she wanted. In my response to the lazy princess, I explained to her that in my line of work, being talked down to and disrespected was normal; but to have someone I worked with let their dog defecate in front of me and make no attempt at a cleanup was the most condescending act I had ever witnessed on the job. This begged the question, Who was harassing whom? You see, I can be eloquent when I have to be. She was not amused and forwarded the email to the superintendent, claiming harassment. This backfired on her. He was wondering why the teacher had begun to email me with her allegations.

The pooping did not stop; even I had bagged the droppings in colorful plastic bags to show her where her dog was doing his business. So I took it to the next level. I bagged the feces one morning and tied the bag to the side-view mirror of her car. This was the last straw. She demanded that something be done. Do you know the school district spent an entire day looking at the tapes from the security cameras to see if I had done this? All they had to do was ask me. I would have saved them a lot of time and effort. That is when our meeting was scheduled. It would include me, her, the principal, and the director of buildings and grounds. It was an absolute joke. All I learned from the meeting was that the teacher in question had a gag reflex that made it hard for her to smell feces, even though she had three children at home. I am sure their dirty diapers smelled worse than her dog's gift to the front yard. Even her waterworks at the meeting could not cause her to get her wish. I was still employed at the school. I really hope she is one of the few who reads this book!

The summertime at a school district is very interesting. The teachers have all gone home for vacation, and except for a few people like office staff, the custodians and maintenance staff are all that are left. This means one good thing–less cars to dodge in the parking lots. It is definitely a more-relaxed atmosphere, and I tended to get a lot more work done during this season. We, on grounds, would be assigned one or two college students every summer to help us with our daily duties. These kids were always past graduates of the district and were only eligible for work while they were enrolled in college. The amount of training they got at the school district left a lot to be desired. Every summer, the boss would sit the new kid down and play a video. The video was on how to operate a large riding mower. That was the extent of their training. They were then sent out on a thirty-five-thousand-dollar piece of equipment and asked to mow the district grounds. Every year, bar none, there was an accident. One of the side decks would be torn off, or something would be hit. It was just a matter of time. I am surprised that during my ten years at the school no one was seriously injured or killed.

The college help was great, for the most part. Many of the guys were hard workers and appreciated the opportunity to earn some cash for college. There are always exceptions to the rule. One of our summer kids used to spend his lunch hours smoking as much pot as a former roommate of mine. His eyes were so closed when he would finish with lunch, you could have blindfolded him with dental floss. Everyone knew this was going on, but nothing was ever done about it. It must have taken too much effort to remove someone from their position. Yes, I am being sarcastic; but in my opinion, a major catastrophe was averted with this particular kid.

During my final four summers at the district, a student I had once coached in baseball was given the job. He was wise beyond his years and knew how to get me going. He once witnessed our boss running up the ramp outside our shop to jump in his work truck. If you ever worked for this guy, you knew he never ran for anything. The college kid watched him trot by and asked me if our boss was excited because he was going out to lunch.

During my fourth year at the school, I was given the opportunity to coach the junior varsity baseball team. For years, I had wanted to get back into an active role in the sport that I fell in love with as a young child. This made for some very long days, but it was well worth it. I will talk about my coaching experience in another section later on.

My days from March through June would start at 4:00 a.m., and the earliest I would arrive at my house would be 7:00 p.m. That is, of course, if we are just talking about practice days. Games would be a different story. There were evenings when I did not pull into my own driveway until ten o'clock at night. The amount of pay I received basically covered my gasoline for the months I coached, but I would have done it for free. That is, if I could have gotten my wife to agree to it.

Our big week for sports fields every year was homecoming week. All the fields had to be at their best, and that meant a lot of extra red paint. The reason for it was that the school colors happened to be red and white. I really enjoyed this week at work. Rolling stripes in the fields and adding our team symbol to the middle of the fields really spruced up the campus every October. This one particular year, my boss decided that he would paint the football helmet design at the fifty-yard line of our field. While he was doing this, I was numbering the yard lines by using a template. I had started at the goal line and was moving across the field, marking every other line. The *G* was painted white then outlined in red. I then continued to the ten, twenty, and so on. The problem arose when I got to the forty-yard line. There was the big red helmet! He had painted it on the forty instead of the fifty. For a split second, I thought I had screwed the numbers up. I double-checked what I had done, and sure enough, the helmet was on the forty-yard line. I have never seen the color come out of someone's face as quickly as it did when I relayed the news to him. His response was, "Oh, well, just leave it there." There wasn't enough time to fix it. He was correct in his response. Painting over the mistake in green paint and repainting the template where it belonged would have been too time-consuming and would not have looked good. Green paint never really does the trick in covering up a mistake on a playing field. My answer was to put something on the opposing forty-yard line. After a few minutes of arguing about it, we decided to freehand a red football. Surprisingly enough, it came out quite nice. I think the football field got more compliments on the field that year than any hour. The coaches, players and administrators loved the look of the big football on one forty and the helmet on the other. Little did anyone know that it was done to cover a blunder that was done earlier on that same day.

If you know anything about maintaining athletic fields, you know that the fields that take the most work are baseball and softball. No other fields have a skinned surface; therefore they do not take as much time or effort. Try explaining this to a coach of another sport. Another problem that arose was the location of our baseball field. It happened to be in a direct line of site to many of the teacher's classroom windows. The criticism got worse after I started coaching baseball. The comments ranged from "He was on that field all day, getting it ready for his game" to "All he cares about is baseball."

Spring in Western New York is very wet. Spring sports season starts in early March, and the last thing coaches want is to practice indoors. It is frustrating, to say the least. Tennis and tract are no-brainers. Once the courts and track are dry, it's game on. Lacrosse, baseball, and softball are more challenging. The snow finally melts, and then the spring rains come. I often wondered if we were ever going to get on the fields, let alone play games. You just had to weather the storm. Each year seemed to be a repeat of the year before. Getting the fields dried and in playing condition was probably a contributing fact to the aneurysm in my upper aorta that nearly killed me in the fall of 2011. I probably would have worked and coached at the school district until my retirement, but the winters were brutal on my recovery from open-heart surgery, and I set my sights on moving to a warmer climate.

In the summer of 2013, after an exhaustive two years of searching, I landed a job at a small university in central Virginia. So in August of that year, my wife and I packed the two dogs and uprooted ourselves for the journey to the other side of the Mason and Dixon line. I should correct myself by stating that I moved down. My wife would join me in February of 2014, after the house was sold. She did come down for a few days that August to help me find an apartment and get set up for the next stage in my adventures in groundskeeping. My apartment was an unfurnished place to sleep, eat, and shower. I had a television and a mattress. The two dogs and furniture moved down in January to give me someone to talk to and keep me from sitting on the floor, as I had been doing since the trip. One of the employees actually came to my apartment after work one night to look at my computer problem I was having. He entered, took a look around, and said, "I'm sorry, R.A." The blank space was reminiscent of the apartment I had rented in the winter of 1988 in Royal Oak, Michigan.

In my new job, I was working for the athletic department. Playing fields were the top priority, and the transition was a quick one. After all, I had been taking care of playing fields for the last ten years. Little had I known that I was going to be working for the most paranoid, negative, worst communicator I had ever worked for. It was so discouraging and uncomfortable to work for this man that I did something I have never done in my life. I quit a job without having another job lined up. After the first ten minutes of starting my new job, I knew it would be a challenge for me to work for him. He started with his first question. Do you wear deodorant? I thought he was joking. Little did I know, he wasn't. He explained that he really didn't like it because it burned his underarms.

Now, you have to understand that this guy is in his late thirties. He is not a child, but I learned really quickly that he had the maturity level of one. He threw fits constantly, when things weren't going his way or when he thought he had been wronged. I mean a full-fledged fit–throwing tools and stomping his feet. It was hard to watch. The only solace would be to reenact the event with the other employees later on in the day. That wasn't even the worst part. He had a bachelor's degree in turf management, so I thought I would learn a lot from him. In my two years at that job, he taught me absolutely nothing. He had been employed at the university for seven years. Before that, he had worked as an intern for a few pro teams, so this was his first real job, and he was unprepared and unwilling to become a good manager.

My stubbornness to make the move to Virginia kept me plugging along and keeping a positive attitude. However, dread would appear every time he was in my general area of work. Suddenly, I was having trouble thinking for myself. His managing style was to tell anyone under him that they didn't know what they were doing. He was also the master of the blame game and pitting employees against one another. Things I had done on the job for years suddenly became hard to accomplish because of his constant second-guessing and general negative attitude.

The worst part about it was his lying. He never said that he didn't know something. He would simply make up an answer or exclaim that the question you asked wasn't important. I picked up on this fact very quickly, and to prove my point to my fellow workers, I would prove it. One day, I told them to watch and listen to my question toward him. In Upstate New York, the white grub is a very serious problem in turf care. So my question to him on this day was a simple one. I asked him if grubs were ever a problem on the fields. His answer did not surprise me. "No," he explained, "the winters are too cold here." I had all I could do to keep from laughing. It was what I had predicted to the other guys. I learned something that day. It is colder in Virginia during the winter months than it is in western New York.

If he didn't know how to handle a job, which was often, he would give the job to one of us. His instructions would be, "Do what you think." After the job was completed, the second-guessing would start. "I wouldn't have done it that way" and "You don't know what you are doing" were just par for the course with a guy who should have never been hired for the job. I can honestly say that he had zero qualities that made him a good fit for the job. In fact, three weeks after I started the job, an employee who had worked for the college for seventeen years decided he had had enough and quit. It was a pattern that had been ignored by the human resources department, as well as the upper management, who were overseeing his position. Employees would not last working for him. The turnover was constant. The problem was that he was allowed free reign with no checks and balances. In fact, one of my fellow employees had gone to the human resources department to complain about our treatment a few months before I resigned. There answer was, "Apply for another job with the university, and get away from him." I was reading the writing on the wall.

Ultimately, after I quit, a change was made. My ex-boss was removed from his position and now has replaced me as a grunt with the athletic department. It was too late for me, but hopefully, the problem is solved for future employees with athletic grounds. He used to tell all of us that no one cared about the gardens around the playing fields. The only thing we were to worry about was the playing fields. Therefore, the common areas become an overgrown mess. I learned very quickly that it was just his way to try and get management to let him hire another employee. That was the way he did things. He figured that if things were not getting done, management would see it as we didn't have enough people working in our department. It was embarrassing to drive by these areas on the way into work. I can only imagine what a prospective student and his family thought when they visited campus for the first time. The campus grounds staff would make sure to point it out to us at every opportunity. They enjoyed rubbing it in, and they also knew who we were dealing with.

To a man, every one of them had had a run-in with our boss. If you parked too close to him in the staff parking lot, he attacked you. If you were using a piece of equipment he needed, he complained. I cannot recount how many times they would tell me things like; "I don't know how you work for him" or "I am surprised no one has ever punched him for treating his employees like he does." It was a well-known fact that everyone hated this man, and sometimes, I think he may have enjoyed that.

A baby pacifier once found a way on his desk, and he spent the entire week trying to find out who had placed it there. He was threatened with physical harm on at least five occasions during my tenure. Where else can you work and get away with that in today's society? I once witnessed him crash our tractor into the fence surrounding our soccer field and pretzel it into scrap metal. Instead of taking the blame for it, he said it was because he was angry at another employee for being in a spot on the field that he was not supposed to be. He would misspeak all the time when giving you directions. Later on, when he would ask you about it, he would tell you that he never said that and that you needed to listen better.

If I wasn't a witness to all this mayhem, I don't think I would have believed it. From the coaches to the student athletes, everyone knew what he was like, and nothing was done about it until after I left. I can tell you one thing–my first morning waking up no longer employed there was the most I had felt relaxed in two years. You see, I had made that decision on the morning of June 15, mainly due to the fact that my stress level was not going to allow me to make it to my next birthday, which was only two weeks away. This seems to be a good lead-in to the next section of my book, which will explain the health issues I faced in this strange trip to my fiftieth birthday–one birthday I believe I had made it to because of my decision to leave the wackiest and worst boss I had ever had.

HEALTH ISSUES

I HAVE NEVER been sick a lot. I was one of those kids who never was absent from school. Even as I entered my work life, I never took many sick days. Sure, I had cases of the flu and colds, but it was a rare event when I felt too ill to go to work. One exception to this was a bout with an intestinal virus during winter break in my sixth-grade year of school. I was so sick for a couple days, I had hallucinations. One of these involved my older sister. I was in bed on the top bunk, battling a fever, chills, and throwing up at an alarming rate. She was walking in the main hallway outside my bedroom, heading into the main upstairs bathroom. She seemed to be floating in my mind, and the bottom of her body was attached to a canoe. It seemed so real at the time and scared me half to death. I can still picture it in my mind. It was like my imagination had blended with reality for a short time.

My first bout with any health-related issues as an adult was at the beginning of 1997. I had only been married for a few months, and I was awakened one Saturday morning with an awful pain in my lower back. It was my introduction to the wonderful world of kidney stones. For the next fifteen years, I would have one or two of these a year. I am a "six foot three, two hundred and ten pound" man, and let me tell you, these little guys have brought me to my knees on many occasions. The doctors could never pinpoint why I was getting so many of them. My thought was that I have never drunk enough water, and the dehydration I have put my body through has caused the problem. It has been a few years since my last one, so hopefully, I have outgrown them.

I never had to have any surgery to remove them, but I did spend a few nights in the hospital for treatment. What I mean by treatment is being given an intravenous saline solution and painkillers to allow for the process of passing them through the system. This is where I met a friend of mine. His name was morphine, and I can understand why soldiers who have been administered this on the battlefield have become addicted. Once it is administered, your troubles are over. The pain is gone, and you enter a state of euphoria. Everyone in the hospital suddenly became my best friend. Every female nurse I referred to as my wife's name, and the comedy show was on. I still do not know if the hospital staff was laughing at me or with me. Under the influence of morphine, I really didn't care.

I become a real expert at pinpointing when I was about to have a kidney stone make it's break from the kidney and travel down the urethra on its journey to my bladder. A few hours before the journey, I would feel a dull pain in my testicles, and this would tell me that I was in for a long day or days. My largest and hardest kidney stone to pass was measured to eight millimeters in size. I still have this stone in a plastic container and have showed it off a few times to the nonbelievers! I know it seems like a weird thing to have hung on to, but it is part of my history. My regular doctor asked me the question after the eight-millimeter monster was passed at my home. "You passed a stone that big at your home and didn't have it surgically removed?" he asked. "You are either the toughest man alive or the craziest" was his response to my answer of yes. I tend to think I lean more to the latter.

One thing passing this many kidney stones gave me was pain tolerance—something I would definitely need in my battle with an aortic aneurysm. It happened innocently enough. I was at my yearly doctor's visit in October of 2010. My doctor performed his routine tests. He listened to my heart, did the dreaded prostate check, and asked the normal general questions about my health. Then, he asked the question that I had never heard and that would change my life. "Have you ever been treated for an irregular heartbeat?"

"Never," I answered, and he responded by saying that something sounded off when he had listened to my heart. He then ordered an echocardiogram to be performed the following day. While I was receiving this test, in my gut, I knew the lab technician had found something. As I lay on my side, he kept looking and measuring one section near my heart. It was a beautiful fall day as I drove home to my house to spend the rest of my day with my aging and kindhearted Lhasa apso named Gretzky. After an afternoon spent raking leaves, I received the phone call from my physician at about five o'clock p.m. My doctor was blunt and to the point. "You have an aortic aneurysm in your upper aorta," he explained. For a brief second, I was terrified, but he explained that he would monitor its size and that I shouldn't worry about it. As I ended the phone conversation, I joked that at least I now knew what was going to kill me. He didn't laugh. I guess my sense of humor isn't for everyone.

I now had to play the mental game of putting this diagnosis out of my mind. It was hard to do; any little twinge or skipped heartbeat now took me to the land of paranoia. It seemed I had a ticking time bomb inside me, and there was nothing I could do about it. Little did I know at the time, the bomb would go off in just over a year from the day it was diagnosed. I then went back to the coaching and work life as I had done before with one exception–I began to have fake heart attacks at every opportunity I had. I would clutch my chest in front of workers who knew of my predicament and exclaim that I was having chest pains. I sure got a kick out of it, but I was usually the only one who did. The secretary at the athletic director's office would laugh, but she was uneasy about it. I guess it didn't help that I would ask her things like, "If I die soon, would you come to my funeral?" It was just my defense mechanism to use humor during tough times. It was something I picked up from my years as a cemetery worker, I guess.

The summer of 2011 was a tough one for my wife and me. We had never been able to have children, and we lost the closest thing we had to one in July of that year. We both are dog lovers, and in the spring of 1999, we got one. He was a little Lhasa apso named Gretzky, and he would become a huge part of both our lives for the next twelve years. The poor guy was diabetic and half blind by the time he was eight years old, but what a wonderful dog he was. He was a legend in our neighborhood, and on every walk, he seemed to sense how special he was to everyone. He began to slow down during his final two years of life and, in July of 2011, had developed inoperable cancer. My wife and I had one last special week with him that ended with him being put to sleep. We had both taken the week off to let him know how special he was to both of us. It was a hard decision to end his life, but we both did not want to see him suffer at all. After all, he had a tough life full of insulin shots, and we both thought he had been through enough. That Friday was one of the most heartbreaking days of my life, and the wimpy side of me took over. I couldn't even accompany my wife to his final veterinarian visit, and my heart had broken.

I was a mess for a long time. I am not the kind of guy who cries, but I was full of tears for a few weeks after that. Since my wife had never seen me so sad and upset, about a month after, she suggested an idea. We made a trip to the local animal shelter and came home with not one but two Shih Tzu–an eight-year-old boy named Logan and an unrelated three-year-old named Badger. These two guys have been bringing joy to our life ever since. They also would play a major role in helping me recover from the impending open-heart surgery that was, unbeknownst to me, just around the corner.

Another summer went by, and I had my yearly exam with my doctor at the end of October. I received great news at the latest visit. The aneurysm had not grown in size. "Keep doing what you are doing" was what my doctor told me as I left his office that day. I was in a great mood as I left, and for the first time in a year, the aneurysm was not front and center in my mind. The mood was short-lived, as I would find out in a few short weeks.

It was now November 7, and the cool weather had come to Western New York. I spent the entire day on a tractor aerating the athletic fields on campus. I left work and drove the twenty-eight miles home at the end of the day. The two dogs greeted me, like they always did, and I took them for their daily walk. I then proceeded to check my email for the day, and that is when it happened. As I stood over my two dogs, I suddenly began breathing heavily, and I could feel my heart beating extremely fast. It felt as though a small drummer boy was performing inside my chest cavity. I then felt the pain that would bring me to my knees. It felt as though a knife was ripping through my chest and exiting out through my open mouth. It was so intense; I dropped to my knees and blacked out for a time. When I did wake up, my dogs were licking my face. They must have thought that their daddy had come down on the floor to play with them. My last thought before I had hit the floor was, "God, please do not let me die like this." I did not want my wife to come home and find her husband dead on the floor of the computer room.

As I regained my senses, I realized I was not dead but that I was going to have a hospital stay. In retrospect, I should have called an ambulance at that point, but I didn't want to panic my wife, so I came up with a plan. I called her and asked her if, when she got home, she wouldn't mind taking me to the emergency room. I tried to play it off as a precautionary visit, but in my mind, I knew I was in big trouble. As she made her trip home from work, I decided to get cleaned up for my visit with a fresh shower. Although the pain had not subsided, it had not gotten any worse, and I was doing my best at ignoring it. Little did I know that at the time, I had suffered an aortic dissection, and my life was teetering on the brink.

On our way to the emergency room, I confessed to my wife that I thought that there was something going on with my aneurysm. She was angry with me for not calling for an ambulance, but little did she know how much danger I was really in. I reported to the nurse at the emergency room that I thought that my aneurysm had ruptured. This fact was taken very lightly. I think it was probably due to the fact that I had walked into the hospital and not been wheeled in. I paced in the waiting room for over an hour, and the pain in my mouth and jaw was becoming unbearable. When I finally was taken into a bed, the wait continued for another several hours. I was pleading for the doctors to give me an MRI. My wife was doing the same. I heard her tell a physician that her husband never complains about pain, so if he is complaining, something is definitely wrong. What finally did the trick was a conversation I had with the emergency room physician. He came to my bedside and asked me how I was doing. "Not great," I told him. I then asked him if he could get me a pair of pliers and bring them to me.

"Why do you need them?" he asked.

My answer stunned him, but he now knew how much pain I was in. I wanted to pull out my own teeth. That got the job done, and shortly thereafter, I was being wheeled to get that MRI. The results were quick and serious. A doctor came into my room and told me that I had suffered an aortic dissection. She then told me I was being transferred to another hospital where I would be having open-heart surgery. After hearing the words come out of her mouth, I was almost relieved. After all, hadn't I been telling these people for hours that I thought my aneurysm had ruptured? I realized right then that having known I had an aortic aneurysm had saved my life. Who knows what I would have been treated for if I hadn't insisted they check my aorta?

The transfer was quick. I was strapped to a gurney and wheeled to the ambulance within minutes from hearing the news. As I look back on all of it now, I must have been in shock, because I never felt nervous or scared. In fact, I never shut up on the ambulance ride to the other hospital. It was time for my stand-up routine. When the question was asked if I had ever been administered anesthesia, my answer was, "No, but I did stay at a Holiday Inn Express last night." My wife never found any of my attempts at humor amusing. She was a mess, and I did my best to assure her that I was going to be all right.

There was never a doubt in my mind, especially after I met the surgeon. He was cocky, confident, and needless to say, he was the guy I wanted to open me up. He walked in and said, "You are in bad shape. If I perform this surgery on you, there is a seventy-five percent chance you'll make it. If I don't do it, you will be dead by morning." Straight and to the point, just the way I like it. After all, I was a C student in college, so a 75 was a good enough grade. It was closing in on midnight on November 7. My next memory would not be for another three days. When I think back on what was done to me, this was a good thing. The surgery to repair my aorta would take eight hours, and it would require an induced coma. It is truly amazing what medical science is capable of these days. Twenty-five years earlier and I wouldn't have made it through the night.

I went in on a Monday, and my memories started coming back to me on Wednesday. My first memory was sitting in a room surrounded by people I knew. However, it was strange; I recognized them, but their names escaped me. I knew I was in a hospital, but I truly did not know why I had drain tubes and an oxygen mask attached to me. It was like coming out of a dark cave. Soon, the names started coming back to me, and I realized why I was there. I was in so much pain and felt so week; I figured my hospital stay was going to last a long time. I was wrong. I would be going back home on Saturday and would be going back to my job in three months.

One of my first memories was of my mother-in-law. You see, in order to perform the procedure to fix the aorta, I was placed in a coma for several hours. As only my mother-in-law could do, she asked me the question that was on everyone's mind. At least, it was the question that was on her mind. "Did you have any near-death experiences while you were in the coma?" Although my answer was no, we still get a kick out of the question and its timing. It would seem that no funny stories could come out of my stay in the hospital, but they did. When my wife asked me what I would like to eat on that Wednesday of my rebirth, my answer was pickles. Was I pregnant, or was this the first thing that had popped into my suddenly alive brain?

My mother and youngest sister showed up right around my first attempt at walking. I had been in the bed for a few days, and I guess just standing up released all the gasses that had been hiding in my body since Monday. As I stood up in front of my sister, all the air was released from my buttocks. We both began to laugh, and this created a problem. Whoever said that laughter is the best medicine never was recovering from open-heart surgery. The pain was unbearable but I couldn't stop and neither could she. I recall my words to her were, "Please don't make me laugh," as I hugged myself to avoid my ribcage from becoming disengaged from my body. Don't get me started on my first sneeze. I knew it was coming, and I knew it was going to be painful, but there was nothing I could do about it. The pain after the sneeze was agonizing, but it must have looked hilarious to anyone who witnessed it.

A question from one of the nurses also surprised me. "Would you like to urinate on your own?" was the question she asked. "Sure" was my simple answer, not having any idea what was meant by the question posed to me. She then reached and pulled the catheter from my private area in a slow, deliberate motion that brought tears to my eyes. I had no idea I even had a catheter at the time and am glad I didn't know. It would have given me time to think about the question and plenty of time to dread the result. Soon, the rest of the tubes were removed from my body, and this included the drain tube connected to my chest cavity. Here is my warning to anyone who ever has one of these connected to them. They are not pleasant when removed. My guess is that it's because your skin has started to grow around the actual tube. When removed, it feels as though your insides are being removed with the rubber tubing. The doctor who removed the drain tube looked at my face as he was doing this. He must have seen the pain I was in and asked, "That didn't hurt that much, did it?" My answer was to tell him to remember that question if he ever had one removed from his body.

Early on that Saturday morning I was asked the question, Do you want to go home? I could hardly contain myself. The doctors and nurses had been great, but I really wanted to leave the cardiac unit behind me. When the doctor who had asked the question left my room, I dialed the phone in my room and heard the shaky voice of my wife. It was about seven o'clock in the morning, and I had forgotten about caller ID. My wife had seen the number come up on our home phone and had been terrified to answer it. She said that I had scared her to death, but I had to call. I wanted to make sure she brought my favorite Yankee hat with her to cover up my five days of pillow head.

It was a beautiful early fall day in Rochester when I was wheeled to the car. It felt like I hadn't been outside in years, and the rush of cold air in my face immediately tired me out. It would take a few weeks for the stamina to come back to me. The next few weeks of my life were spent in a recliner, in and out of catnaps, and the occasional bathroom trip. The surprising thing to me was how my two dogs acted during these first few weeks. They slept with me during the day and were the most gentle of creatures. They were sure not to step on my chest and never asked to go outside. I definitely buy into the theory that dogs have a sixth sense about things. They returned to their out habits of jumping on my genitals and barking at every opportunity soon after they sensed I was out of danger.

I was scheduled to return to work in late January of 2012, but that was moved back after my third occurrence of an irregular heartbeat. It was called atrial flutter, and it had been controlled with medication during my hospital stay on two different occasions with meds. Now that I was at home, my physician wanted to handle it with cardioversion. In laymen's terms, my heart would be shocked back into its normal rhythm. It was one of the longest weeks of my life, waiting for the procedure to be completed. Anyone who has had to deal with atrial flutter can attest to this. It feels like there is a canary in your chest cavity. The irregular heartbeat makes your heart feel as though it is in a constant state of quivering. It is damn near impossible to sleep, and I was as irritable as I have ever been. On the morning of the procedure, I had to fast and try to stay calm until 3:00 p.m. Finally, when the procedure was completed, it was over and done before I knew what had hit me. The technician explained to me what was going to happen. A small camera would be sent down my esophagus and check to make sure there were no clots in my heart. If everything was good to go at this point, my heart would be shocked back into its normal rhythm.

As I always do when I am at the doctor's, I asked a lot of questions before the procedure started. I wanted to know if anyone had ever woken up during the procedure. The technician responded, "All the time, in fact, sometimes a sweet old woman will sit up in bed and curse like a sailor, only to return to snoring a few seconds later." I was enthralled by this statement, and I asked him if he wouldn't mind videotaping my procedure so I could enjoy it later. Of course, the answer was no, and I never found out if I had sat up and yelled out. I sure would have like to see a video of that!

The procedure went off without a hitch. I remember the doctor counting down to zero, and that was it. My next memory was sitting on my couch at nine o'clock that evening, watching television. Where had the day gone? I asked my wife if I had gone to the hospital for my procedure and if I had gotten anything to eat. Her answer was yes to both questions. She then proceeded to tell me that I had asked her to take me out for dinner, and while we were there, I hadn't stopped talking. I have no memory of anything that happened after the doctor's final countdown to zero. I still wonder if I sat up after being shocked to curse. I never saw any video evidence to the contrary.

This little procedure to get my heart back into a normal rhythm moved my comeback to the school district back a couple weeks, but it allowed me to enjoy the Super Bowl before returning. The answer to the question is yes, I am a New York Giants fan. If you remember correctly, I grew up in southern New Jersey, in the heart of Eagles country. Why am I a Giants fan, you ask? The answer is in the size of my head. You see, when I was a four-year-old child, all I wanted for Christmas that year was a football helmet. My parents decided to take me to the store. They explained to me that Santa Claus needed to know my size if he were to bring me a helmet to put under the tree. We went to the store, and it was loaded with Eagles helmets and a few of the other big teams at the time. If I remember correctly, there were a few Dallas, Pittsburgh, and a few others sprinkled in. I tried on every one, and they were all too small. I discovered that day that I had an unusually large head for a four-year-old boy. We were about to leave the store, and I spotted a blue-colored helmet tucked away in the corner. Much to my amazement, it fit my larger-than-normal head perfectly. Yes, the team was the New York Giants, and I have been a fan ever since.

Being a fan of this team where I grew up caused many an argument in the lunchroom. That brand-new helmet sure looked good under our Christmas tree in December of 1969. Anyway, I enjoyed the Super Bowl in 2012 more than usual. My team ended up winning their fourth championship, and it took some of the sting out of the last three months. I would say it took me at least six months after returning to the job to fully feel like I was back to normal.

It was now the beginning of February, and the new baseball season was just around the corner. Was I capable of putting in those long days from March until June? The answer would come on a forty-degree day in March of 2012. We had just started tryouts for the school's baseball team earlier in the week. This is normally the most exciting week for me as a coach and the most dreadful. At the end of this first week, I always find out which players would be called up to the varsity team and which players did not make the cut. Cutting a player was a very tough job for me as a coach. Looking a young kid in the eye and telling him he would not be making the team was very hard for me to do, especially when it involved a player who had been on my team the season before. I would have loved to keep everyone who tried out on the squad–but unfortunately, it is a numbers game, and there are only so many spots to fill on a baseball team. This particular season, I never made it to that point. On the morning in question, I was marking a practice lacrosse field and realized that my heart was racing, and I was drenched in perspiration. Remember, it was a forty-degree day, and painting fields was something that had become second nature to me. I realized at that moment that I was getting worn down, and it would be a wise decision for me to resign from my position as coach.

I returned to my shop to call the athletic director. He was not available, so I spoke to his secretary, whom I considered a good friend and still do. I told her of my plans and that I needed to talk to her boss about them. In the middle of the phone call, my voice began to crack, and I began to get emotional. This was something new to me. Other than a death in the family, including my dog, this is something that never occurred to me. I had to end the phone call as I wept like a child for several minutes. Coaching that JV baseball team meant the world to me, and realizing that my health was keeping me from doing that had broken my heart. The athletic director understood my position and promised that if I was well, I could return to coaching the following year.

I ended up coaching first base for all the home games that year for both the varsity and JV teams. It kept me around the sport I loved and allowed me to fully recover from my battle with open-heart surgery. In hindsight, it was a smart decision to give up the reins of my team. I really don't think I would still be around to write this book if I had put in those long days so close to my dance with death. It wasn't like my boss was picking up the slack and putting in a full day of work.

COACHING

WHEN MY BASEBALL career ended during my college career, there was a void left in my life. After college, playing in recreation softball leagues had sort of filled that void, but it wasn't the same. Soon after my career started at the school district, I approached the athletic director and told him of my desire to coach high school baseball. I figured that the opportunity would never present itself. Teachers normally held these positions and, in fact, could force a coach out of a coaching position if he was not a teacher in the district. I never understood that policy. First dibs were given to teachers working in that district, no matter what. Fortunately for me, JV baseball is not a very glamorous coaching position. There are not as many articles written in the local papers about this level as there are at the varsity level. This was the opening I needed to get back into the game of baseball.

During the late winter of 2008, the position of JV baseball coach was empty, and no teachers in the district had any interest in filling it. I was contacted by the athletic director and asked if I still had an interest in coaching baseball. My answer, of course, was yes. Thus began my career as a baseball coach. I had no idea what it would amount to at the time. I figured I would be moved out of the position by a new teacher at some time down the road, but I had to give it a try. So in March of 2008, I threw myself into the world of ninth- and tenth-grade boys. There were some who had the same dreams I had in high school and others who were more suited to become stand-up comedians somewhere down the line.

During the first week of practice, all the boys from grade 9 to 12 are together. The coaches then decide which players will start the season on JV and which will become varsity players. I was starting my career at a disadvantage. I had no idea what the kids' names were since I wasn't around them as a teacher would be. I was very quiet that first week, and I am sure most of the players must have had no clue what this new coach was all about. I was taking the opportunity to see what kind of team I could assemble.

What I saw that week really scared me. I wasn't sure what I was witnessing, but it was not a baseball team. I had watched the team play during the first four years I worked for the school, and to say they struggled would be putting it very mildly. The baseball program was not very good. There was some talent here, but there also was a lack of fundamentals and commitment. After that first week, I had the fifteen kids that would make up the first team I would ever coach. After my first week alone with the team, I figured it would be the last team I would ever coach. To say the first week with them was rough would be putting it mildly.

Before the weather breaks and fields become playable, the JV team practices in a gym located in the elementary school. Tight quarters are not conducive to baseball practice, but I made the best of it. I ran drills designed to teach fundamentals and basically ran them into the ground with conditioning. By Thursday of that first week, I thought I had made a huge mistake, deciding to coach. It seemed like the vast majority of kids were not listening, and I wasn't making any headway. On that same Thursday, I told the kids how I felt, and I also told them what they could do about it. If they wanted to have a teacher who just rolled baseballs out onto the gym floor and let them do what they wanted, all they had to do was go home and complain to their parents. I also told them that the days of mediocre baseball at this school ended today. Some of the kids cursed me under their breath, and when practice ended that day, I didn't see the smiles that had been there during the first couple days of our separate practices.

I went home and told my wife that I had been very hard on them, and I would probably hear about it the next day. I was sure that my days as a baseball coach were coming to an end. My idea when it comes to baseball is simple–the game is supposed to be fun. However, that doesn't mean that there is not work involved in playing the game. I was trying to instill that in my players but, in my opinion, was failing miserably. I went to work the next day, fully expecting to be called down to the AD's office and replaced as coach. The call never came.

I was working on cleaning the parking lot at the elementary school and was approached by a woman who worked in the cafeteria. She approached me and referred to me as "that baseball coach doing a great job." I looked at her, very puzzled, and asked her what she meant. She told me that she was longtime friends with one of my players' mothers, and she had told her what a great job I was doing. She went on to tell me that her friend's son loved what I was doing. I was shocked. I explained to her that I thought the kids hated me and that my coaching career was short-lived. She told me that this kid thought I was great and that I really cared. She went on to say that I was really helping regain his love for baseball that had been lost over the last couple of seasons. I can't begin to tell you how surprised I was at hearing all of this.

Soon the weather would break, and my coaching talent would be tested in real games. This would also be my introduction to dealing with today's parents. It's possibly the main reason why coaches decide not to continue doing the job. I had a couple of advantages going for me when it came to this factor. The main factor was that I was not the varsity coach. JV parents, for the most part, are not as into the spotlight as much as varsity parents. I can't even begin to imagine what sports like varsity football and basketball coaches go through. Another thing I had going for me was the fact that I lived almost thirty miles from the school district. There was not much of a chance of my running into one of these parents on the weekends or during the evenings.

This factor was the main reason why a friend of mine had resigned as the head coach for the girls' varsity basketball team. He lived in town and was constantly being asked about playing time and so forth. The tipping point was a visit he had from a parent. His doorbell rang one night, and there stood another teacher in the district who happened to have a daughter on the team. He wanted to discuss his daughter's playing time right there on the spot. This parent was not only a teacher in the district but also a coach. I wonder how he would have felt if the tables were turned and someone had done that to him.

This is not to say that I didn't have any parents that overstepped my boundaries. In fact, one afternoon, I was in the shop, sharpening mower blades, when I heard a voice call out, "Mr. Fields, could I speak to you for a moment?" He wanted to know if I had a problem with his son. I had no idea where the conversation was going, but his son happened to be a great kid, and I enjoyed coaching him. He figured I did have a problem because his son was not playing as much as some of the other players. I have always played everyone on my teams, but obviously, certain players are going to get more playing time than others. I never minded discussing playing time and other things with parents; it was just the location that needed to be adjusted. My working hours should have been off-limits without me ever having to say anything. I couldn't imagine how embarrassed I would have been if my father had complained to a coach about my playing time back in the day. This was just an example of how things are different than they used to be.

One difference that made my job easier was cell phones. You may wonder why this would make a coach's job easier, and I will tell you. It is the bus trips. I would rather have today's player occupied by his music or texting than I would have them moon a carload of nuns. This is not to say that some of our road trips did not get out of hand. Most of the noise came from the JV softball team we traveled with to most of our road games. These girls were crazy, loud, and obnoxious. (And I am being nice.) It is no wonder that the school had to give extra pay to the bus drivers who made these extra trips. I doubt that the parents of these teenage girls knew how they acted during these trips. I can only hope they did not. Some of them were downright vulgar. The school would have had to pay me double to coach this group.

That was not the most vulgar language I heard in my tenure as coach. This title would go not to a parent but a grandparent of one of my kids. This kid was a funny kid, but not a very good ballplayer or student. He cut class, he skipped practices, and he generally did not put in much effort. My main rule was if you skipped practice the day before a game without a good excuse, you weren't playing in that game. I did not have many rules, but this was one of them. During this particular game, we won in extra innings, and the player in question did not see any action. I am sure he never explained to Grandpa that he had missed practice the day before with no excuse. I had finished putting the field to bed for the night and was walking the equipment bags to my jeep parked in the school parking lot. As I loaded the jeep, Grandpa unloaded on me, with Grandma right at his side. He never said anything directly to me, but his words were obviously directed at me. He let fly with the full arsenal of four-letter words, basically telling me that his grandson should have played and that I was ruining him for his varsity shot the following year. With Grandmother looking on, he went on for about five minutes. I am sure that my no response to his words angered him even more. After about five minutes, he and his wife angrily drove off. Thus the old saying, "You can't please everybody."

The player in question never showed up again. He never tried out for varsity the following season and was subsequently arrested for shoplifting a couple years later. I am sure Grandpa probably blames me for his demise. If you are reading this, you are probably asking the question, Why would anyone want to coach? I can tell you that the good still outweighs the bad when it comes to coaching. Sure, there are negatives, but that is the same for anything. The thing I miss most about moving to Virginia is coaching those guys. We finally got to start actually playing games in my first year, and I was looking forward to seeing how good we were against competition.

My tenure started pretty rough. We lost our first five games, and most of them were never in doubt. It was hard losing and tough seeing the kids go through it. Then it was like someone turned on a light switch; we started winning. We were tied in our sixth game, and that is when the parents were introduced to my other side. I had my first argument with an umpire. The team was really starting to battle, and we were finally in a close game. The game was tied, and a base hit would win the game for us in walk-off fashion, or so I thought. There was a base hit to right field, and I sent the runner home. After all, it would take a perfect throw to the plate to get him. As I followed the runner from third to home plate, I noticed their catcher was blocking the plate without the ball–a no-no in high school baseball; and a rule change at the major-league level in subsequent years has also made it illegal. I already started yelling, "He's blocking the plate. He's blocking the plate!" The throw nabbed our runner, and the game was into extra innings. I lost it.

I don't remember throwing my hat, but my players described my actions to me later. I argued vehemently with the umpire to no avail. I came into our dugout, still angry, and screamed, "Let's go!" My team ran back onto the field, and we ended up losing again. This time in extra innings.

I was aware that I completely lost my temper in front of all the parents and was embarrassed by this. Now I was worried about my job security once again. I was again waiting to be called to the carpet the next day. I did not have to wait very long for a phone call. It was the varsity coach calling me at my home. He asked me, "What happened?" I asked him how he found out. Apparently, a small group of JV parents waited for the varsity bus and told him about the fireworks at our game. The funny thing is, they were not angry–they were elated. They told the varsity coach how pleased they were that they finally had a coach who cared so much and that he backed up their kids. I was shocked, and I think my response shocked him. I told him, "Hell, if that's all it takes to get the parents on my side, I could have a tirade every game."

Of course, I was joking, and my run-ins with the men in blue were few and far between during my coaching career. That does not mean my intensity for baseball ever let up. I cannot remember actually sitting in the dugout once during the entire time I coached. I always admired those managers that could sit in the dugout during the game, but that was not me. I lived and died with every pitch, and I am sure that might have had something to do with my aneurysm. When it comes to baseball, you could say that I am wound pretty tight. I really got a great feeling when my guys did well out there and started to win games. You see, my wife and I were never able to have children of our own, like I have stated before. The boys I inherited during those springs from 2008 to 2013 became surrogate sons to me. In some ways, they each have a place in my heart, even the one whose grandfather cursed me in the parking lot.

We ended that first season with a .500 record. I figured it was growing pains. I was just getting my feet wet in the coaching profession. The second season would test my love for the game more than I could ever imagine. It was very exciting going into that second year. A couple of my really good players from the year before were returning as sophomores, and I believed we had a very strong group of incoming freshmen. We started off well and won our first game that season. The rest of the season was a battle, as we were only to be victorious two more times. The reason was team chemistry. These kids argued on the field, they argued at practice, and the season quickly fell apart. I was finding myself counting down to the last day–something I never thought would happen to me. Yes, I did not want to go to the baseball field for the first time in my life. I remember after one game sitting in the locker room when I asked one of our captains the question, What am I doing wrong? His answer stunned me. He answered, "Coach, no one cares about baseball on this team as much as you do." His words definitely hit home.

He also asked me if I was finished coaching after this year. Although the season had been a grind and I had lost twenty five pounds, I couldn't end my career with a three-win season. I would have always looked back and thought I had failed. Besides, the last two weeks had showed me something. We were in each game. We just seemed to always find a way to lose.

My chance to coach baseball the next year almost came to an end anyway. The athletic director who had given me the opportunity to coach had resigned. About a month before the season, the new AD called me into his office. "I think we need to shake things up," he exclaimed. His plan was to move the modified coach up to the JV position and move me down to the modified level, which means coaching seventh and eighth graders. Due to a lack of any interest in baseball coaches throughout the district, I held my ground. Since I believed I had done a decent job with the kids and hadn't had any complaints filed by parents, I felt it was unfair to move a teacher into my position. I would have made the move, but I called his bluff. I told him that I would resign as coach but would not be bounced out of the position. He decided to keep things the same, and I prepared for what I thought would be my last year as a baseball coach. By the time the following year came around, I would be offered the varsity position and would have the best record and most enjoyable season to date.

I changed the way I approached coaching. If they didn't care as much as I did, I would have to accept that fact. I developed more games to implement in the indoor practices. We might not be any good, but damn it, we were going to have fun. That doesn't mean that I stopped working them. To the contrary, I think this team may have been in better shape than my first two. Something funny happened–the team responded. They seemed more excited to play than before. I had changed my approach. Instead of dwelling on the negatives, I became a much more positive coach, and it became fun again. We ended up with a 13–7 record with a team that I felt had less talent than its two predecessors.

One of the team's shining stars was a very likable short left-handed pitcher. At the time of this book being written, he is a division 1 pitcher entering his junior year. My trips to the mound when he was pitching were a joy. He would say things like, "You wouldn't have to come out here if someone could field a ground ball." He was speaking the truth. The beauty of it was that he never showed anyone on the team up. It was just a private conversation between a player and his coach. Some of the funniest memories I have about coaching took place during meetings on the mound. Just the year before, I had been told by a pitcher on the team who had just walked two straight hitters this classic. "Coach, if I walk the next guy, you can take me out."

I laughed and said, "Thank you for giving me permission to do so." The player who uttered that memorable line just completed his college degree and pitched four years at a division 3 school.

One of the other leaders on this third JV team was a stalky, fun-loving third basemen. The problem was, he had an interesting habit. He would vomit before every game. The big problem was getting him to do it somewhere other than the trash can in the home dugout. About halfway through the season, I finally got him to do it in the away dugout. I am sure it was not the classiest move on my part. He was also susceptible to nosebleeds. This one particular game fell on a Saturday morning. We were cruising to an easy victory when it happened. The problem was, I only had nine players for that game. I was feverishly trying to get his nose to stop bleeding between innings when we took the field for defense. It wouldn't stop easily, so I had to delay the start of the inning. I called time and slowly walked toward our pitcher. He looked at me, dumbfounded. "Why are you taking me out? We are killing them," he asked. I had to explain to him that we were tending to the daily nosebleed, and I simply was buying more time. Minutes later, our infielder returned with two cotton balls stuffed in his nostrils, and we went on to complete another victory in a most enjoyable season.

Unlike the previous season, I was sad to see it end. The players had enjoyed the ride, and a couple of them have told me that that season had been the most fun they had ever had playing the game. It definitely reenergized the old coach from South Jersey. During the following winter, the varsity coach resigned, and I was offered the position. What a difference a year makes! I declined the offer. I was in the perfect situation. I have always thrived more being behind the scenes than front and center. I also felt that I was at a level that I could still teach these kids that love for the game that I still had.

Being diagnosed with the aortic aneurysm had also been a factor. I wanted to stay away from any added stress brought on by the added pressure of winning at the varsity level. Do I think I would have done a good job? Yes, I do, but I honestly think I had my dream job.

The fourth season of JV baseball was an interesting one. That is, when we got to play. It was a wetter-than-normal spring in Western New York, and the team had only a chance to play thirteen games that year. To say we were a young group would be an understatement. There were only three returning players from the talented group from the season before, and the team consisted of seven players who were still in eighth grade. Besides dealing with the maturity level, I was also dealing with a parental group that was by far the most competitive group I had ever been associated with. Each one of them seemed to know how well their child matched up with the other players on the team.

I also had to deal with something I like to call stat padding. Anyone who has ever coached baseball understands that it is a tough job to coach and keep the stat book at the same time. To the credit of the parents, someone would always volunteer to keep the book for me each game. This particular season, I had one father step up to be the unofficial scorekeeper for the season. The problem was, his son never committed an error and led the team in hitting. I say this, of course, with my tongue mounted directly into cheek. Any time his son made contact with the baseball, the resulting stat in the book would be a base hit. He failed to realize that after games, I would review the scorebook and make the appropriate changes before posting the team stats online. One day, he questioned me on why his son's batting average was only .277 when he had it at .560. My answer was simple. I explained to him that I actually was the official scorekeeper of the team, and my stats were actually the stats that mattered. This also went on at the varsity level. I never understood how he felt this was helping his kid at all, but I will talk more about social media in a later section.

I felt we overachieved that season and ended up breaking even in our win/ loss record. During the last inning of our last game, I had a funny exchange with a player I had coached for the last two years. As he prepared to take his last at bat in his JV career, I jokingly told him he was the worst player I had ever coached and was glad we were finished. As he walked to the plate he turned and said, "Well, you were the worst baseball coach I ever played for, so it worked out." The wide-eyed umpire looked at me and asked if that was the way we talked to one another on this team. When I responded, "Yes," he just shook his head and crouched back behind home plate to finish out the game. I would venture to guess that my coaching style was something new to him.

As I stated before, the next season was one that I skipped due to my health issues. I was still around both teams during home games, but I missed the day-to-day coaching very much. The 2013 season was a fantastic experience. The team played great all year and, with a record of 14–5, easily won the league title to make my swan song season one to remember. I could tell a few days into practice that it was going to be that kind of year. The team was a confident bunch and showed up to work and had fun every day.

Just before the start of the season, I had begun my search for jobs in a warmer climate. I actually had flown down to South Carolina to interview for one such position. Although I was not offered the job, I felt that this very well could be the last spring coaching baseball at the school. The players knew I were looking to make the move, and they had no problem telling me what they thought of it. Several of the players who would probably be returning to play JV in 2014 threatened to come find me down south if I didn't come back to coach the following year. It was nice to be appreciated by them, and I don't think they ever will know how much being around them meant to me. One great thing about this new age of social media is that I have been able to follow their careers since I left them two years ago.

Our season had ended, but baseball was not over yet for our varsity team. I coached first base for the sectional playoffs, as I had done in previous years when my season was over. Remember that little left-handed pitcher I had coached a few seasons prior? He was now a senior and voted our section's player of the year. We ended up winning the school's first sectional title in its history. What a goodbye gift that was. The memory of those kids celebrating on the bus when we were led back into town by a fire engine will always have a place in my heart. Nothing like seeing their hard work pay off. My coaching career officially ended in August of 2013, as I made the move to the place I call home today.

TRYING TO HAVE CHILDREN OF OUR OWN

O NE OF MY older sisters uttered the line about my difficulty having children that I will never forget. She said, "Wow, imagine how much fun you would have had in college if you would have known then that you were shooting blanks." My family always seems to find humor in every situation, and this was no different.

After a couple years of being married, my wife and I had decided to start a family. After finding that traditional methods had not worked, we sought the help of the professionals in the health-care industry. At the end of this three-year stretch of taking off my pants for a number of doctors, a trip to the dentist almost resulted in me stripping. It had become second nature to strip, and I had to remind myself that dentists were more concerned with the other end of my body. It started with testing to see if my sperm count was high enough to impregnate my wife. I never gave it much thought to how these samples were obtained until this process started. The first couple of times I had to present a sample, I chose to bring it in from home. I found that this was a big mistake. You see, the sample has to be tested within a half hour, and the stress of driving the boys to the hospital was enormous. I found myself praying that every traffic light was green and that I could find a parking spot close to the office where they were to be delivered. It was like becoming part of a science project.

Since my count was low, the chances of us becoming pregnant was greatly decreased. My wife and I had to have everything be perfect for it to work, and we failed to achieve the results we were looking for. We decided to take it to the next step. Before this next step occurred, however, I would be run through a series of tests. The first one of these tests involved a sonogram. I reported to the area of the hospital where the test was to take place and quickly realized that I was the only nonpregnant woman in the area. I felt like a celebrity of sorts.

First off, the hospital gown did not come close to covering my back side. As I walked down the hallway to have my private parts x-rayed, it felt like a million eyes were on me. I felt like I was taking a walk of shame. Did these people think I was lost or just a very ugly woman? I felt like sprinting to the room where the test would be administered.

I had two jobs to do during the test. The first job was to stand there as it was taking place. The second job would involve a towel and a severe case of embarrassment. I had to hold my twig away from the berries so the two nurses could examine the inside of those berries. The entire test must have taken about a half hour, but it seemed like a week as far as I was concerned. Of course, the nurses were young and beautiful. I remember thinking that I used to imagine things like this as a younger man, but now I was wishing to be anywhere else but here. As I stood over them, I was imagining baseball highlights in my head instead of looking down at their beautiful, ponytailed blond hair. They ran that little machine over the berries and talked to each other about the results like I wasn't even there. The only conversation they would have with me was to tell me when they were going to apply more cream to the area and that it would feel cold.

Finally, it was over, and they told me to wait a few minutes alone. As I sat in the room alone, I happened to glance at the computer screen at some point. The monitor said, "Mr. Fields' right testicle." I could only hope this would be erased before the next pregnant women entered the room. What if, by chance, the next women in possibly knew me?

There were more tests to go through, and for some of them, I can honestly tell you, I have no idea of what they were trying to accomplish. One of these tests took place at an urologist's office. I entered the waiting room and was at least thirty years younger than any of the other patients waiting. Then it happened–I was recognized. An elderly gentleman approached me and told me he was sure he recognized from somewhere. I politely told him that I had no idea from where, but I was constantly being told that I looked like someone. As I continued to wait for my turn, the man shouted from across the waiting room, "I know now, you were the guy who buried my wife!" He was right, I was working at the cemetery at the time, and this guy had recognized me. I don't think I have ever been more depressed in my life.

My turn came, and I was told to disrobe and place my feet in the stirrups. You heard me right, the stirrups. I now have some ideas what the female readers of this book have to go through. I was then asked by the doctor, "Would it be all right if one of my students sits in on the visit?" I answered, "Sure." I figured they had to learn sometime. It was another pretty blonde in her twenties. I was then handed the towel. I knew what my job was. I was on my back with my feet up, and the testing began on the berries. They moved them, they used calipers to measure them, and the whole time this was going on, there was the blond head of the trainee inches from them, trying to learn the trade. I was beginning to think I was living a nightmare. There came a point during the testing where I overheard the doctor tell her that the average size was twenty. When mine were put into the calipers, the measurement was thirty. For a split second, I wanted to pop up from the bed and ask her out. I thought better of it. I am not sure if the joke would have gone over very well, and I was in an awkward position.

After all these tests were completed, they came to the conclusion that they had no conclusion. There was not an answer for why my count was low. My wife and I turned to the next option, artificial insemination. I would have to have my swimmers ready at a moment's notice. I had decided to produce my samples at the hospital where this was to occur. If memory serves me correctly, we tried this option about five times without achieving the desired results. Since insurance will only cover the process up to three times, we changed our insurance policy three times to try and become parents. The first time I produced the swimmers to be used, I was directed to a private room. It is a very nerve-racking experience. I was constantly thinking that someone would come in and catch me like I was breaking the law. The nurse instructed me that there were videos that I could watch to help the process. I was embarrassed, but I figured I wasn't the first man who had used this room to do something that boys are told will make them blind. I finally finished and was eager to present the small plastic cup to the attending nurse.

Problem was, when I exited my private room, there was no one to be found. The place was deserted. I desperately wandered the hallway, looking for someone to take my swimmers from me. I found an elevator and headed for what I thought would be the lobby. Perhaps if I found my way there, I could find someone to direct me to where I needed to go. The bell chimed, and the elevator doors opened. I stepped out to find a maintenance worker in the middle of welding. Sparks were everywhere. I turned to look at the elevator door and, above it, noticed the words "Service elevator, official use only." I had taken the wrong ride. At this moment, the maintenance worker had noticed me and removed his welding mask. "Can I help you?" he asked. "You are not supposed to be down here." *No kidding*, I thought; but in my embarrassed state, I could not find the words to answer him. I quickly jumped back into the elevator and returned to the place where I had come. I was stepping out of the service elevator when I ran into the nurse who I had been looking for. "Where have you been?" she asked. I wanted to ask her the same thing, but I just handed the jar to her and got the hell out of there!

The next hospital I had to deliver the boys to did not have one of those rooms. I got to the office that day, and the receptionist asked me if I had my sample. After telling her that I did not, I was ushered to a private room again. Unfortunately, this private room was the broom closet. Apparently, this hospital's patients always brought the samples from home. As I entered the closet filled with mops and brooms, that uneasy feeling accompanied me once again. How was I supposed to perform and give them a sample in these conditions? For one, the lock on the door was nonexistent. What if the janitor walked in during my performance? Would I be arrested? This was a bad situation, but what were my options? I began the process by leaning against the door, for security purposes. Now, I have an extremely strong imagination, and I was going to have to delve into it. I began to look at the mop head like it was the flowing hair of a beautiful woman.

Then it happened. I began to hear the staff's conversation. It was a Monday, so everyone in the adjoining room was telling stories of the past weekend. I learned that one of the nurses was divorced, and it was her ex-husband's weekend to see the children. Another nurse had gone to a local amusement park and had a grand time. Had they forgotten what I was trying to do in here? I must have been in that closet for over an hour when, to my surprise, I had completed the process. I then had to make that all-too-familiar walk of shame. I didn't help that the closet door had not seen any grease in decades. As I walked by the now-full waiting room, the nurse behind the glass blurted out, "Do you have your semen sample, Mr. Fields?" Everyone in the room looked up from their reading material and stared at my now-reddened face. Needless to say, I could have used a bucket of ice when I hustled myself out of there. I would not ever use that closet again.

The next two trips to this hospital involved me using the public restroom down in the lobby. When the question was asked from that point on, my answer was, "Yes, I did bring my sample from home." If they really thought about it, it would have been impossible for make the trip from my house to the office in under a half hour. I guess they just didn't want to know. Thank God for me, the lock on the bathroom stall worked, and there were no more mops to look at.

Unfortunately for us, it was not to be. The science project had ended, and we were resigned to the fact that we were not going to become parents. I always thought I would have been a good father. I also wanted to hand down my larger-than-normal baseball cap collection to someone. A golden lining to this is the fact that a child would not have to go through watching their father battle for his life. I can only imagine how tough that is on a child. It was tough enough when I was in my late twenties. This all just goes to prove one thing: you really can't plan anything. This includes having a family. You just never know what life holds in store for you down the road. I was a guy who never planned on marriage. I never thought a woman could put up with me for the long haul.

BOSSES

I N A WAY, this section could be titled Marriage. After all, I have spent more time with some of these people than I have my actual wife. Unlike the marriage to my own wife, most of these have ended up in divorce. What I will attempt to do in this section is give the reader some insight into the type of people I have worked for over the years. You must remember when reading this section that, although I am describing certain types of bosses, most of these people could be placed in more than one category. In fact, a few of these characters of my past could be placed in every category of boss I will describe in this section.

The first type of manager is what I like to refer to as the Fortune 500 boss. This is the guy who manages like he is working for a major business juggernaut. Fortunately, I have only had to deal with this type of boss on a couple of occasions. You have to remember the type of work I have done over the years. These two guys just could not relate to the blue-collar workers who they were managing. They would show up to work in a suit and each carried a leather briefcase. A fellow worker once joked that the case must have been filled with comic books for him to read in the office. These two just couldn't relate to us, and I do not really think they wanted to. We, on the other hand, did not and could not relate to them. They both liked to lay more responsibilities on their workers without much foresight.

Lucky for me, I encountered both of these guys before computers and the internet became a mainstay in the office, as they are today. You see, as many of the bosses I have had to date, they never had to come up through the ranks as in a lot of cases. They were both so well-spoken and could talk a good game, they were both rushed through the system. It is extremely hard to respect someone who doesn't know what you are going through. In my opinion, the internet would have made it even worse. In today's world, people can get the answers to their question on how-tos by simply clicking a mouse. I am constantly telling people I work with, especially the younger ones, that the internet is full of opinions. Just because you can read about it doesn't make it the right way to do it.

One of these guys was very intimidated by me having a degree in forestry. He would contently let me know that he never had the opportunity to get a college degree. He was another one of those guys who assumed that if you went to college, your family was wealthy. This fact, coupled with how I got along with the other guys at the job, made these two resent me. They just never trusted me, and it was made obvious. I once overheard a conversation between this type of boss and another member of management. He believed me to have so much power over the other workers that if I told them to walk out of the job, he believed that they all would follow me out the door. He just never understood that most guys relate to others who struggle as they do on a daily basis and talk to them like men, not peasants as he tended to.

The trust issue came to a head when the sale of a business where I was working was beginning to take place. The sale was going to become official in about a month, and the boss was worried. He figured that a lot of guys were going to quit when the sale was finalized, and he was worried about theft. A few of the middle managers, like myself, had keys to open up the business each morning. I still believe the reason for this is that the Fortune 500 type of boss cannot be bothered with showing up to work before 9:00 a.m. He told me directly that I needed to turn in my keys because he was afraid of "things disappearing before the sale." I obliged without any hesitation. I also thought this was going to happen, and I knew the distrusting boss would figure I would be the one with the sticky fingers.

It happened anyway, of course. Guys were stealing five-hundred-dollar spreaders and spray units right out of the warehouse. They were the guys he trusted. The ones who had toed the company line for years. You know the type– the guys who give answers that they think the boss wants to hear instead of answering honestly. Giving an honest answer was something I was taught from day 1; however, the Fortune 500 type of boss always thought it was negative to not respond in the way he wanted. The same guys who I used to see nodding in agreeance with him during meetings were the same ones who robbed the company blind at the end of its existence. Somehow, he probably still thought I had found a way to gain entrance to the building.

The other Fortune 500 type had once accused me of stealing a spreader that had been tossed out. He told me his theory was that I was probably thinking about starting a business, and I needed the equipment. I laughed in his face. It's something I wouldn't suggest you do to the Fortune 500 type of boss. After all, the business world is a serious place to these guys. I told him that "if I was going to start a business, I would be sure to buy a decent spreader, not the twenty-five-dollar piece of junk that we had in our shop." This is one time the internet would have worked in my favor. He could have looked it up while I was standing there and seen that I was correct.

The most entertaining part of having the Fortune 500 boss was the yearly holiday party. He would show up with wife in tow, looking like they were on their prom date. The rest of us, happy to get a free meal, would come with our dates for the night. Most of us were living paycheck to paycheck, so we didn't own a suit. This fact must have appalled the Fortune 500 boss. Guys were digging into their free meals like they had never eaten before. It was really fun to see him squirm. He just didn't understand that those grueling twelve-hour days were tough, and if we had a chance to let our hair down for a while, we were going to take full advantage of the opportunity.

The Fortune 500 type is never one for timing either. He would schedule meetings at the most inopportune times. The guys would come back after a day in the hot sun and be told to stay put. We were having one of the boss's mandatory meetings. We all wanted to go home for the evening but were forced to sit through a long-winded pep talk that usually had the same topic. Gaining more customers was his favorite subject. Nothing was ever brought up by him involving keeping the customers we already had. I, to my detriment, would always try to break up the sour mood at these meetings by finding humor in something he said. This was never taken well. Usually, the result was a tongue-lashing by the boss in front of the whole group. I never understood why a jab at humor was always deemed as a bad attitude by this type of boss. I will say this, getting the entire room to laugh was always worth being abused by the type of boss I found to be my least favorite.

The next category of people I have worked for never utter the phrase "I don't know." These are the artists of providing false information to everyone under them. Although annoying, this type of boss can be rattled quite easily. These people, for some reason, always think that answering "I don't know" is a sign of weakness. They are very predictable, and I have always like pressing them to answer questions just to see what they would put out there.

One occurrence of this occurred in my job in the southern side of the country. I picked up pretty quickly that I had this type of boss. I announced to one of my fellow workers of my plan to get a made-up answer instead of an "I don't know." I approached my boss with my witness in tow and put the question out there. My question was, Do you get a lot of grub damage on your turf in Virginia? Remember, I had just moved from Western New York. His answer was "No." Fair enough, but it didn't stop there. He continued to explain to me that the temperatures were too cold to allow the pests to be a real problem in Virginia. He just couldn't help himself. He had to inject some made-up facts to the answer to make his point seem factual. We had a good laugh about his answer later.

I have gotten a little better at holding my laughter until a later time. I like to call it a gift, but sometimes, I lose that gift at the most inopportune times. A question was once asked to this type of boss, and his reaction was worth the angry stare he gave me after my outburst of laughter. A question was asked of him during a job that didn't really pertain to what we were doing at the time. He tried to answer it in his normal way. Halfway through his made-up answer, he started struggling. I think he realized he just should have said, "I don't know," but those three words were not in his vocabulary. Instead, he turned on the employee and lambasted him. "Why are you worried about that?" he asked in an irritated tone. "That has nothing to do with what we are trying to accomplish," he screamed. I had to walk away with another employee as we both began to laugh. He had been caught not knowing an answer–something he must have been taught was a sign of weakness. He chose to turn his anger on another employee instead of just using those simple three words that should be in everyone's vocabulary. I would definitely have a lot more respect for a manager who would admit he did not know the answer instead of always having an answer.

This type also has the tendency of throwing his education or experience in your face. When pushed, you always have to hear about where he gained his degree or the number of years' experience he has had in doing the job. My father had always told me, "Remember, there is always someone better than you" as it pertained to sports. This is also the case in the working world. The problem with this type of boss is, they believe that no one has the experience or education they have to do the job better than they do. This is why I believe that they always have to have an answer for every question posed to them.

I had come to this job with a ton of experience in the playing field and turf grass industry. This was the reason I was hired, or so I thought. I was constantly told that I did not know what I was doing. I believe this was just the intimidation factor gnawing at this type of boss. I had used a spreader for many years with good results, but the one with the turf degree knew it all.

One day, I was applying fertilizer to one of the fields, and he approached me to let me know of his concerns. He was worried about the coverage I was getting with the fertilizer. Getting inconsistent coverage when applying fertilizer can lead to different shades of green or streaking on the field. In his opinion, which was always fact in his mind, I was not getting good coverage and was probably going to streak the field. He asked me how I knew if I was getting good coverage. My answer did not please him and his normal reaction came out once again. "You don't know what you are doing." What was my answer to him in the first place? I told him that I was allowing my fertilizer to hit the wheel marks made from my last pass, and this would ensure that I was getting good coverage. He angrily walked off the field, mumbling as he usually did.

Well, this time, the gods of timing were on my side. If you have ever worked in the landscape business, you know that there are education seminars a few times during the year. They consist of professionals who are in the business and college professors putting out information and allowing new products to be viewed, etc. It just so happened that a week after our meeting on the field, we had one of these seminars nearby. One of the topics was on the proper use of a spreader and fertilizing techniques. I couldn't have planned it any better. A professor with a doctorate in turf was teaching the hour-long course, which was really just a review for most of us in attendance. He then posed the question, "What is the easiest way to know you are getting good coverage with the application of fertilizer using a rotary spreader?" Some random answers were thrown out there, but I knew the answer and just waited. He then looked at the gathered crowd and said, "The best way to make sure you are getting good coverage is to hit the wheel marks of your last pass." Sometimes, things just work out. I really wanted to take off my shirt, exposing my scar, and wave it over my head in celebration; but a little fist pump was all I could muster at the time.

There is another obvious tactic this type of boss always seems to use. Whenever a job is given to them that they have never had to do before, they use the hand-off technique. This is when you or another coworker are called upon to get the job done from start to finish. The man who never admits when he is wrong will magically disappear until the project is completed. This is when the second-guessing always takes place. Questions like, Why did you do it that way? are asked. Monday-morning quarterbacking is a staple to this kind of boss. I always got the feeling that while we were completing the task, the boss was busy back at the office, researching internet sites to come up with his idea of what should have been done.

The one thing I could always count on after the internet age started was that bosses never delete their computer history. I was amazed at some of the things I discovered in their absence. At one of my jobs, we had a golf outing at the end of the school year. It was always a fun event and also gave me the opportunity to stick it to the man, if you will. There is always something so satisfying about beating boss at something. During the days up to the event this particular year, we noticed that the boss was spending more time than usual in the office. I had a hunch on what he was doing. You see, this type of boss does not like to look like he does not know what he is doing. After all, he is the one that always has the answer. I waited for the chance to be alone in the office and reviewed the history on the computer. He had spent hour upon hour looking up videos on golf. He simply had typed the words "how to hit a golf ball straight" into the computer's search engine and had his answer. Imagine getting paid to watch online videos of golfers hitting the ball and providing tips to the novice player. That is what was being done here, and you know what, it didn't work. I think he lost a dozen balls during our nine-hole outing the next day. I couldn't resist. I played pretty well that day, and one of the guys asked me if I had practiced. My answer was directed toward the boss in a very subtle manner. I answered, "No, I just searched how to hit a golf ball straight on the computer."

He had to know what I had done, but he never mentioned it and took his defeat as expected. "Boy, I haven't played this bad in a long time." The typical response of someone who will never admit they don't know and can never admit when they are wrong. In fact, they oftentimes try to slip the blame on someone else for their inadequacies. One of these examples occurred when my boss misplaced his cell phone. We had spent most of the day laying sod on our baseball field. Every member of the crew was there and was told several times during the job that they didn't know what they were doing. My boss's go-to phrase, as stated before.

At the end of the day, he had placed his cell phone in the cupholder on the service vehicle I was driving back to the shop. Of course, the fact he had done this was lost on me. Somewhere during my trip back to our home base, the phone had fallen off my ride. We were busy putting tools away when he asked me the question, "Where is my cell phone?" Of course, I had no idea and asked him where he had seen it last. That is where his typical attack on a subordinate took place. "I put it in your ride!" he screamed. "You have to be more considerate with other people's things." It was the way he worked. It was never his responsibility; it was always placed on you. Thank God I had matured over the years. An earlier version of me may have threatened his life.

On my way out the door of that job, I did relay this fact to the human resource department. I told them that workplace violence would occur if he continued to act like that toward his employees. Hopefully, they have put some stock in my words. Another shouting scene occurred during the early-morning hours on the job. As I drove in that morning, I had noticed a shovel, rake, and trowel lying on the soccer field. At seven in the morning, I removed the tools from the field and began using the trowel to remove weeds from a flower bed on campus. At 7:45, the boss's normal time to start, I heard a scream from across the parking lot. Apparently, he had been working on a faulty sprinkler system the night before and, since the job was not complete, had decided to leave the tools on the field. "Did you take my tools?" he asked. Knowing that the answer was yes but asking anyway, he again screamed and berated me. "Don't take my tools!" is how he left me.

I screamed after him, "Don't leave them overnight on a field!" These confrontations and uncomfortable situations were a daily occurrence at the job. This was definitely no way to motivate a crew you were overseeing. It quickly became apparent to me and the rest of the crew that when the boss was off, we not only completed more work but actually communicated better and were more efficient. The boss was actually an anchor holding the group down, but according to him, we really didn't know what we were talking about.

On rare occasions, I have had to deal with another type of boss. He is the opposite of the micromanager, which seems to be prevalent in the industry where I have done most of my work. This type is totally hands off. He doesn't tell you a thing. This is the type of boss that you see very little of during the workday. Of course, I cannot count this type when my job consisted of taking care of lawn or tree customers all day long. I was on my own during this type of employment until I returned to the shop at the end of the day. No, this is the supervisor who is supposed to be organizing what needs to be done during the day and is supposed to be part of the crew but is nowhere to be found for long periods during the day. These guys have zero leadership qualities and never come to work with a plan. One of these types would walk into the office every day and say aloud, "What are we going to do today?" This was not in jest; he really had no idea what to do and was just happy to have guys on the crew who were self-motivated and knew what needed to be done. In my opinion as well as others, these types of bosses are just paycheck collectors and never had any leadership qualities that would have made them a viable candidate for the title they held.

One boss in particular had just been in the right place at the right time. He had been a midlevel manager with me at another company prior to being offered his current title. At the old job, he simply stayed hidden from upper management, and his days were spent making coffee stops and reading the daily newspaper. Subsequently, he had landed a job at his current location simply by having a decent resume and education. Since the company he and I both worked for had been purchased and disbanded a few years earlier, there were no employees left to question about his management skill or motivation as a worker.

It became clearly evident to me after my first interview that he had not changed a bit. I was called into the director's office after that interview to have a heart-to-heart chat with my future boss's supervisor. The director told me straight up that I was going to be offered the job. My references were deemed very good, and my experience was also what they were looking for. Unfortunately, that wasn't the only reason they were offering me the job. I was told in a very direct way that since I had worked with this man before, they were hoping I could light a fire under his posterior end. I knew right then that nothing had changed since I had stopped working with him eight years prior to this point. I immediately told the director that I was well aware of his lack of work ethic from my past experience, but I assured him that I was nothing like the man I would be working for.

I left the meeting happy to have gained a decent job. I also left the meeting with the same feeling that seemed to haunt me at most jobs; no one wants to do the dirty work. I was not only carrying the weight of the work at hand but was also supposed to motivate the boss. This, I felt, was sort of a raw deal. Was I really supposed to motivate someone who earned twenty-thousand dollars a year more than I did to work harder? Wasn't that the director's job? I realized at that very moment that my immediate boss and his supervisor (the director) were exactly like each other. They each loved the title they were given, but not the work that should have come with the title.

These two guys also fell into the category of the "blame game" type of boss. This is type of boss who never takes the blame when something goes wrong. I witnessed this several times in action during accidents with equipment. Once, a supervisor of mine who was more concerned with checking texts messages than watching where he was going slammed a tractor into a section of fencing that surrounded the soccer field. Although it was totally his fault by all who witnessed his stupidity, he had a different spin on what actually occurred. He blamed another employee for the mishap. You see, he was supposed to meet the other employee at the soccer field, but he didn't like the side of the field he had entered. He told me that if he hadn't seen the guy on the opposite end of the field, where he didn't expect him, the crash would never have occurred. Shifting the blame seems to make this type of boss okay with any mistake he has made.

Another accident occurred because someone was mowing the wrong field. You see, the boss was so upset that this was occurring, he backed over a large light post he had been parked in front of to check his text messages. Instead of putting the vehicle in drive, he chose reverse. This was due to his anger with the other employee's decision to mow a field that the boss hadn't wanted mowed.

One type of boss who shifted the blame, I nicknamed Godzilla for his total destruction of property anytime he decided to operate equipment. In the time I worked with him, he destroyed three light poles, several lacrosse goals, and had a real talent for tearing soccer nets completely off of their goals. It was amazing to me that he hadn't severely injured or even killed an employee under his supervision. His ideas for gardening were equally frustrating and destructive.

He had a direct plan when it came to weeding a flower bed, unlike most people in the industry. He wouldn't think to dig the weeds out by hand adding mulch; that was way too much work. His idea involved running a string trimmer into the mulch beds. Cutting the weeds down and covering their root systems with fresh mulch was his way of getting the beds to look better. It lasted about one week. The seeds from the weeds he cut down were spread throughout the flower beds, and within a week or two, the weed population had doubled in size. This method of bed maintenance, something I will admit to have never seen before or since, also created a mess on the walkways adjacent to the flower beds. I would drive up to these areas and instantly know that Godzilla had been there. The mulch and weeds on the sidewalks were a dead giveaway to who the guilty party was. I guess Godzilla never carried a leaf blower with him to clean up the messes he made in those movies either.

This was not the only time mulch beds were attacked for no apparent reason. Godzilla also attacked them when mowing the turf around the property. In his mind, it must have taken too much time to actually run the mower around the beds. He was constantly driving through them, leaving ruts from the tires in the flower beds and throwing mulch into the grass he was trying to mow. I never understood how someone who was supposed to be a professional could do such things without being embarrassed.

His destruction was not limited to the landscaping. The spring sports season was also fair game for his attacks. He never was much for walking, so if there was a way to drive on the fields, he was going to do it. One particular spring day, we had a full schedule of games to prepare for, and the weather from the night before hadn't cooperated. We spent most of the day trying to dry our softball and baseball fields for the games that were scheduled for that afternoon. I was finishing up with the baseball field, when I saw the service vehicle full of equipment driving to the upper softball field. I remember thinking, *I hope he is smart enough to not try and drive to the back field.* I was wrong. A couple minutes after this sighting, I saw him walking back to the shop, and I immediately got a sinking feeling in my gut. That feeling was verified when I saw him on the tractor, heading back toward the same field. He not only had created ruts in the outfield grass, he had gotten the vehicle stuck along the third baseline in foul territory. He was bringing up the tractor to try to pull the other vehicle out.

I had an away game that night and had to be on the bus in twenty minutes, so I had no way of knowing until the next morning what had happened. He had gotten both pieces of equipment stuck on the field. Luckily for him, the two vehicles were in foul territory, and both coaches had decided they could still play that softball game. Thank goodness not one of the girls had errantly run into the two large pieces of equipment that were parked conspicuously along the field of play. I can only imagine what the opposing coaches and players thought when they walked back to the field. Our coaches and players, on the other hand, were used to things like this during Godzilla's reign of terror. I again have to believe that embarrassment is something that doesn't exist in the mind of the blame shifter. I sure was embarrassed, and had nothing to do with the fiasco of ruts and mud.

It is funny and sad that that sort of thing is still going on at that place of employment. I have, over the years, received pictures of the destruction that still takes place. In my ten years employed with him, I can honestly say I never remember him or the director taking the blame for any of their mistakes.

In fact, my boss was a notoriously bad speller. He was just not good at it. Even so, he was on the computer at work enough to make up for his lack of spelling by simply looking up words. I don't know if it was laziness or the fact that he really did not care that kept him from using this resource, but one day, it came back to bite him. He had been assigned a work order to paint part of the bus loop in front of the elementary school. The principal of the school was having problems with cars parking in the school bus loop and was hoping some paint in the parking lot could avoid the problem. The boss was assigned the job of painting the message, 15-Minute Parking Use Hazards. It was a simple job, and he only needed to paint the message three times along the curb strip in front of the school. He had performed the task in the morning and returned for his daily lunch break, when the shop phone rang. We immediately knew that he had done something wrong by his reaction. He laughed nervously and said he would fix the problem. He never moved that fast, so we knew something was up. Later, he told us what had happened. He had spelled the word hazard with and extra *z*, and parents were complaining that the school district should at least be able to spell properly.

Instead of taking the blame on this one, he presented a note that had been handwritten by the head custodian of the school. She had written down examples of what they had wanted for parking areas. There were a couple of suggestions, and the boss had settled on the one in question. She had spelled the word *hazard* wrong in her haste, and my boss was quick to jump on that fact. He made sure everyone knew that it was her fault, not his. Once again, the typical response for the blame shifter. How did he fix the problem? Instead of blacking the whole thing out and redoing it, he combined the two letters into one big *z*. I laughed at the sight of the word *hazard* every time I saw the word painted on that black top. It sure did stick out like a sore thumb from that point on.

These two guys were just meant to work together, I guess. In fact, I was recently blamed by the director for something that happened recently; and I have been gone for over two years. About five years ago, the school district had decided they wanted to remove an island from the front entrance. It made sense; the island contained a tree and a little turf and was surrounded by curbing. The removal of this island would make the job of plowing snow a lot easier and more efficient. I was given the job of removing the tree, and the town would be responsible for the pavement process. I showed up the next day with a chainsaw in hand to do the job that probably would have taken about an hour or so. At that moment, the director stopped me. He immediately told me not to take the tree until everything was scheduled with the town. About once a month, for three years, I called the director to ask him about the tree removal. "I keep forgetting to call the town" was his response, and the job was never completed. About a year ago, I received a message from one of my former coworkers, telling me that that job had finally been completed. He also let me in on what was said by the director. Apparently, I had been told three years prior to remove the tree and never did what I had been instructed to do. After all these years, the blame is still being shifted to someone else.

The next type of boss I have had the pleasure of working for is the micromanager. This type of boss needs no introduction to anyone who has been part of the workforce. I honestly believe bosses like this have an inferiority complex, and this may be the reason that they chose this as their management style. One boss in particular who managed in this style was relentless. I honestly don't think he had ever had an employee who was as self-motivated as I am and didn't run to him with questions or concerns on a daily basis. About a year into being employed under him, I was called to his office. He had concerns that things were not being completed. I asked what was not getting done. He didn't have an answer for me, so I immediately knew. The answer was that he wanted me under his wing. He needed me to start keeping a logbook of everything that I was doing during the day. He wanted it by the minute not just a list of the tasks I completed. I am quite sure he regretted that request the minute I turned in my first monthly logbook.

I gave him what he wanted in waves. I documented everything from picking up a cigarette on ground to filling the string trimmer with gas. It may have been childish on my part, but it sure was fun. If a stranger stopped me while I was mowing the grounds, I documented it to the second. Of course, bathroom breaks were not off-limits either. If I could go back in time, I would have written in my journal if the visit had been for number one or number two. I also would have documented the number of hours and times of the day I had actually wasted filling out his journal. I am thinking I possibly wasted one or two hours a week making sure the micromanager had his thumb over me.

Another thing he loved to do was write out elaborate instructions for jobs any groundskeeper with experience had been doing for years. If there was an area he wanted seeded, the instructions usually went something like this:

1. Bring all equipment and tools to area to be seeded (topsoil, fertilizer, rakes, grass seed, and water supply).
2. Clean area to be seeded of all debris and weeds.
3. Rake in new topsoil, and make sure area is level.

4. Lightly sprinkle seed over entire area with grass seed, making sure that seed is distributed evenly over the entire area.
5. Amend soil with fertilizer.
6. Cover seeded area with straw and water evenly, being careful not to wash away grass seed.
7. Continue to water on a daily basis until desired turf is attained.

This was just one example of the lists he would come up with. They were laughable, and some were even posted in our shop for entertainment value. All he had to do was let me know that an area of the campus needed to be taken care of, and it would have been done. There was absolutely no reason for this. The one reason I could come up with was that this was the way of a micromanager.

His monthly walks with me around the tiny campus were also noteworthy. First off, I had to carry a notepad and make sure I wrote down everything he said. These were orders directed at me from the supervisor himself. We would walk, and he would point out things around campus that he would like addressed. You must remember, there were gardens everywhere and also a large fishpond on campus that I was to take care of. This campus was small, but it did keep me very busy. We would walk, and he would find things that ultimately needed attention, like picking up candy wrapper along the road and pulling weed out of the rose bed. I had all I could do to contain my laughter. The property could be 90 percent weed free, and he would pick out the one weed he could find and that piece of trash that probably was thrown out of a car window five minutes prior to our walk.

Lists were not just for this type of boss. The non-micromanagers were also very fond of these, especially when they were planning on taking a week off from work. They were always a treat and contained nothing that was not on my radar. One boss in particular was very happy to spend an entire day before he left compiling this ridiculous novel. He was not one of the bosses that had a plan at all, but seemed to have one when he would be absent from work. The list was everything to do for the week. It included things that were obvious, like to mow and string trim the entire district and keep the flowers watered. The funny part of this list was that before I had started working here, the boss's idea of a flower bed was a yew bush with a maple tree growing through it. He had not even made a small attempt to beautify the campus, and here he was telling me to make sure the gardens were taken care of during his absence. The things on the list were all jobs we took care of every week, with no direction from the boss. I believe this was just his way of wasting another entire day on the computer during working hours.

I also worked with an employee who had become a slave to the list while our boss was away. He would constantly find it during the week and check off each job that had been completed. I told him that the list was just a guide for me. I was in charge for the week, and he shouldn't worry about the list. My attempt to stop him from checking off everything we did that week was to no avail. I tried hiding the list in the shop, but he kept finding it. Every time I told him what we were doing that day, he wanted to know if it was on the list. I decided to take the list out of the equation altogether. We were at lunch break on Wednesday afternoon when he asked to see the list for what seemed to be the one hundredth time during that week. I stood up and slowly walked to where I had hidden it. I then held it above my head and, looking at him, exclaimed, "This is what I think of the list." I then proceeded to rip it into a million pieces and deposit it into the garbage can. He was shocked and scared. What was going to happen when the boss returned and went over what we had done in his absence? He was so worried that he looked at me and demanded to see the copy of that list that he was sure existed. "There is no copy," I explained. "We don't need that list. We know what we are doing." He didn't buy it. He had been employed at the place longer than I, and the boss's list was regarded as highly as the US Constitution in his eyes.

The funny thing was, my boss never brought that list up once in his meeting with me the following Monday. I am honestly surprised that my fellow employee hadn't taped the pieces of that list back together after I resumed work that day. I am sure that if he had been in charge that week, that list would have had about ten copies, just in case one had been destroyed or lost.

This brings me to the next section of my story. It may seem as though I did not enjoy my career as a groundskeeper; however, I enjoyed it very much. The reason being the job I got to do and the other employees at my level I got to work with.

FELLOW EMPLOYEES

F ELLOW EMPLOYEES ARE probably the main reason my bosses over the years didn't drive me into the loony bin. We shared laughs, long days, and generally loved doing impressions of the boss. Over the years, I worked with people from every walk of life and some really funny characters. I did notice one thing very quickly—it did not take very much time for me to be one of the older guys at work. For my first couple of stops along my journey of employment, I was always the young man on the crew or close to it. By the time I began working for the lawn-care company in 1992, I had become one of the older workers. Lawn care is a tough business, and not many guys want to put up with the long hours and punishment for very long. Most of the men on our crew were in their early twenties, while I was approaching thirty. Most of the newer guys at the job seemed to find their way under my wing. I had trained a lot of them, and they seemed to appreciate my honest answers and fun-loving attitude outside of the workplace.

I have always liked to get to work or any event a little earlier than most people. I never really enjoyed showing up to work at the exact moment the workday started. One of my early arrivals cost me some major damage and a coworker's insurance company quite a bit of money. It was the night of our annual Christmas party, and of course, I was the first one to arrive. I had found a spot in the empty parking lot of the party house where the event was to take place and was quietly listening to the radio. It was a dark, cold night in Western New York, and I was looking forward to watching and taking part in some of the antics that always took place at one of these events. Just then, a car entered the parking lot. It was one of those big land boat cars from the seventies. It made its way across the parking lot at a pretty rapid speed. Soon, the headlights were pointed directly at my small compact car. As the headlights got closer, I remember thinking, *What is this idiot doing? The parking lot is covered in ice.* I soon braced for impact. The car slammed into my tiny car and crushed the driver's side door so bad that I actually had to exit through the opposite door to go find the guy who just ruined my night.

It was a twenty-year-old from work and his date for the night. He got out of his car and quickly apologized for the wreck. "Why were you driving so fast across the icy parking lot?" I asked him. His answer floored me. He told me that when he got there and realized it was me, he got excited and wanted me to meet his girlfriend. Maybe the boss was right. Maybe I could lead all the guys out of the business and shut him down.

To make a long story short, we had fun during the party, and the car eventually was repaired. His girlfriend mentioned to me several times during the night how well I took the whole event. What else was I going to do? The guy was happy to see me. How could I be mad at him?

We also used to take at least one yearly trip to a professional sporting event as a group. One year in particular, I definitely made an impression. We had gotten a block of tickets for an NHL game, and it just so happened that we were in the last row of a standing-room-only crowd. Back in those days, I never really watched what I ate. Fast food was a constant indulgence, and my digestive system let me know how bad it was on an everyday basis. To put it simply, I had gas often. We were seated in the last row during the game, and behind us was a standing row of fans. I spent the entire game floating air biscuits straight up the back of my plastic seat. Hockey games are loud, so there was no need to be silent.

During the third period, a paying customer who was standing behind our group loudly asked a question. "Holy crap, who's been eating the polish sausage?" I immediately bent over in laughter, as did several of the other guys in the group. The man had obviously caught a nose full of my entire game's worth of flatulence. Just then, another man who was standing exclaimed, "It's the guy in the blue-and-red baseball hat. I stood behind him the whole first period and kept smelling it." This resulted in even more laughter from the entire group. I never had to admit to the man that I had been stinking up the joint, but I think we all knew. Thank goodness I changed my diet and don't have that constant problem anymore. It is awfully hard to take a date to the movie theater when you have the feeling you may explode at any moment.

Our boss actually showed us how much of a hockey fan he was that night. He wasn't very into the game at all and had suggested we leave at halftime. I guess in his world, they stopped the game at the ten-minute mark of the second period to let the marching band play. We all had a good laugh about that comment, made even better that it was at his expense.

Of course, I worked with some guys over the years who should not have even been working in this field. These guys complained about everything; it was always too hot or too cold to be working outside. I used to ask them why they did what they did, and none of them could ever truly give me an answer as to why. They hated doing their job and the lack of pay, and the funny thing was, none of these guys were any good at the job. I have learned that, over the years, people who were negative about the working environment and the job were usually at the low end of productivity and quality.

There were few exceptions to this, but once in a while, a guy came into my life that threw this theory out the window. I met him in the early '90s, and he was the epitome of the disgruntled employee. He was near forty years old and seemed even older to all of us. He complained constantly, he was never in a good mood, and he seemed to be on the verge of quitting at every moment. The funny thing was, if you could get by the gruff exterior and his caustic tone, he was a very experienced and knowledgeable employee. He had been doing this kind of work for so long, he had gained a large amount of experience but also a disdain for everything the job entailed and definitely the management aspect of it. He could also turn on the charm when he had to. He was very well-spoken and could explain problems and solutions to the customer as only a seasoned professional could. He was absolutely despised by management. They saw his attitude as bad for morale, which was very understandable if you ever heard the way he complained and moaned in the office.

During the fall of his last year being employed by the company, I had the opportunity to work with him for an entire day. It would be a day I would never forget. It was the end of the year for lawn-care treatments, and we were being doubled up, as was the case every year at this time. The reason for this was the leaves. Once the trees started to drop their leaves, it made fertilizer treatments a lot more time-consuming. Since the lawn had to be cleared first, management felt it was more effective to have two representatives on each lawn. We were working together that fateful day in a rural area about thirty miles from the city.

We were about fifteen minutes from any stores, and I had a nature call. The lawn we were working on was very large, and I had been working in the backyard while he was in the front. I couldn't wait any longer; I just had to relieve myself. So I asked him a question. "Is there anyone home here?" I asked him. His answer was that he had gone to the door and was sure no one was home. I tucked myself between the yew bushes and the house to expel the large amount of coffee from my system. As I was doing this, I happened to look down into the basement window of the home. I found myself looking at a teenage girl in a towel, standing about five feet from me. Thankfully, she was not looking my way. I couldn't get out of the bushes fast enough. If she had looked at me, exposed as I was, jail time would have surely been in my future.

I came around to the front and explained to him what had happened. He was not buying it. "No way," he screamed, "this place is deserted." He always had that attitude toward every story. He was the kind of guy who didn't believe it unless he saw it with his own eyes. I had to show him how close I had become to being arrested for exposure, so after the lawn was finished, I took the bill to the door. I must have stood on that porch for fifteen minutes, waiting for an answer. All the while, he was sitting in the truck, grumbling and shaking his head. I was about to give up when the front door finally opened and the teenage girl appeared to take the bill from my hands. My story had been proven to be a true one, and that is when the fear really set in. What if she had turned to look up for a split second? I had dodged a major bullet. I don't think I ever relieved myself on a customer's lawn after that close call.

We actually made a pretty good team. The winter soon came, and the negative employee was asked to not come back in the spring. It was too bad; he was a good employee. But it was understandable when you looked at it from management's perspective. I ran into him a few years later. He was working for a small company, doing the same job he had done for us. His attitude was exactly the same as I had remembered. He did not have one positive thing to say!

It seems like everywhere I have been employed, there is always one employee just like him. They seem to feel trapped in this line of work with no chance of ever getting out. Over the years, I have learned to steer clear of this type of worker. The job is tough enough without having their pessimism bringing you down even more. The only thing worse than having a fellow employee having a negative attitude is when your supervisor has one; there is no escaping that. You end up making really strange life decisions. In my case, trying to put down my thoughts in the book you are reading at this very moment.

Every place I have worked seems to have another type of employee: the attention seeker. These are the guys who always feel the need to tell the boss what they did that day and get that proverbial pat on the back. In fact, one of the biggest culprits of this style of attention seeking continues it even today in another form. I worked with this guy over twenty years ago, and his daily ritual was to approach the boss and look for that reassurance he was obviously looking for. It was comical to witness on a daily basis, but it was even more entertaining when his fellow employees did impressions of him later. Sales calls involving him were the best. His voice boomed over everyone else's in the office, and he wasn't shy about embellishing his experience to a prospective customer. He was my age, yet when you heard him speak, he had been in the business longer than he had been alive.

The advent of social media must have been beyond his wildest dreams. He is on it at least ten times a day and still looking for those pats on the back; and it is still comical and, in some cases, pathetic. He still works in the field he did back when he annoyed me on a daily basis and still looks for his daily dose of praise. He feels the need to update everyone on how much he got done at work each day, complete with pictures and commentary by him. I really find it quite pathetic that a man in his fifties still needs the assurance that he is a hard worker and does quality work.

Back in the day, his small cubicle was decorated with awards and honors he had received over the years at his profession. I can only imagine what his workplace or den looks like today. I just imagine framed certificates hung on the walls and photographs of completed jobs he worked on. In my opinion, he has fallen into today's rut. I like to call it the struggle for supremacy of the "like" button. You see it every time you turn on the computer–people posting pictures of their meals, selfies, and updates on the last time they suffered from the sniffles. The vanity and self-promotion I witness on a daily basis is truly sad. Even a kind act has to be bragged about to the public.

The problem is, I know the real people behind what is evident on their personal profile. One of the weaknesses of the attention-seeking worker I spoke about was his customer service. He was great at selling the work, but he never followed through on the promises that were made. We were berated constantly by customers that he had done work for, angrily asking, "Why doesn't he return my phone calls?" In this business, it doesn't matter how good you think you are. You will have your detractors. It comes with the territory, and it will happen to everyone. He just could never handle that part of the job. After all, he had all those framed awards and so much experience.

I have even seen this aspect of his life creep into his postings on the internet. He has posted pictures of jobs that were completed under his watchful and professional eye, when it happens. Someone will ask him the question, "When are you going to get to the job at my house?" All of a sudden, you can just feel the mood swing start to shift as it did back in the day. His comments range from "I have been really under the weather lately" or "Work has been really swamped lately, but you are definitely on my list." I cringe when I see these comments. It brings me back to the days when any negative comment toward his work usually turned into an angry tirade full of excuses or bitterness. Back then, I always thought if he spent less time in the boss's office looking for pats on the back and more time following up on customer concerns, he would have made a decent employee.

Nowadays, he spends much of his time on social media, looking for the same attention. I am sure if I checked his profile page this instant, I would be up to date on what he is working on today or the cold he is battling, keeping him from doing the work!

Some of the guys that have this flaw do not have to receive their compliments from the boss. They look for the pat on the back from the nearest employee they find. You can see it coming a mile away. They will approach you or a group of guys, and you can sense it coming. They usually will appear to be out of breath and disheveled. Oftentimes, they would utter my least favorite phrase: "I busted my ass today." Nothing makes my skin crawl worse than this phrase. That phrase, to me, is the epitome of self-promotion. Let someone else tell you—that has always been my argument. What is wrong with just knowing you did your best at work? It has kept me going for almost thirty years in this business, except for the hiccup that has allowed me to write this book.

Some hilarious events at the workplace have taken place when two of these types have come together at one time. The conversation usually goes something like this: "Boy, I really worked hard today." The other employee will answer, "Probably not as hard as I did." I tend to try to break these little attention-getting parties up by letting both employees know how proud we all are of both of them. Sarcasm has not yet seemed to break this type of employee of their tendencies of bringing attention to all the work they have done, but I am still trying. These are the same type of employees who always think they have gotten the short end of the stick when assigned work. In their minds, they always get the hard job for the day. It's really quite fun to watch them complain about how they have the worst job possible.

I recently worked with an employee like this. This was the first full-time job he had ever had, and he had little experience in the work that was to be done. In the experiences he did have, he was very vocal about how the job was supposed to be done. He was definitely a child of the internet, and he spent hours online, researching the different facets that pertained to the job. He was working with a group of guys whose experience dwarfed his in most aspects of the job, but it didn't take long for him to voice his displeasure whenever work was assigned for the day. In his mind, he was always being assigned the hard jobs while the rest of us had it easy. He didn't seem to understand that his lack of experience in certain areas of the job made it impossible for him to be given that assignment on a particular day. He was slowly getting his feet wet in some of the things a groundskeeper takes for granted. He had to learn the basics of the job first before he could move on to the more specialized jobs.

To say he was green when he started was an understatement. He had never run a string trimmer, let alone started one. About a year after he began his employment, we were on our morning trash run when we came upon a crew of city workers mowing and string trimming turf areas along the street. He turned to me and said, "Did you see how that dude was string trimming?"

After I answered his question that I had not, he went on to tell me that the guy was doing everything wrong and had no idea what he was doing. So in a year's worth of time, he had gone from the one with zero experience to the man with all the answers.

This is when the real side of him showed up. I liked to call it his argumentative side. He argued about everything–sports, politics, religion, and the job. Nothing was off-limits. He would question everything that was being done. All you had to do was state your opinion on world events, and he had the answer. It was frustrating, to say the least. He had told me that he never wanted a management position because he never wanted the pressure to make decisions or the responsibility that came with the title. That did not stop him from questioning every decision that was made by his superior. When the boss was absent, I was placed in charge of the other employees. Like clockwork, every time I explained to him what needed to be done, he had another idea and argued his point. We let him know constantly that he had this side to him, and his answer was a simple one. He claimed that he was not argumentative; he was just right. I often told him that he should pursue a job in law. He could get paid to litigate his case in a courtroom instead of giving everyone around him headaches on the grounds crew.

He was explaining to us one day about his new girlfriend. He, of course, had met her online and had begun a long-distance relationship with her a year before. He was finally going to meet her in person and spend an extended weekend with her the following week. I could not wait to get this jab in when he returned from his overdue rendezvous. He returned on a Monday and began to tell us how well the face-to-face meeting had gone. I waited for him to finish when I asked the question that had been milling around in my head for some time. I started out by explaining myself. I asked the question. Had he ever seen those cheesy romantic comedies where there is always that scene where the couple has their first fight? I then proceeded to ask him if their first fight had occurred five minutes into that meeting. It got the laugh I was looking for. Even the argumentative employee had to give me the props on that one.

Over the years, I would have to say that 90 percent of the people I have worked with are people that I would not hesitate to share a foxhole with; but the 10 percent I have talked about seem to have been the most entertaining and, at times, frustrating. Some of the hardest-working people I have worked with are the people in the office. They come to work each day not looking for accolades, just trying to do an honest day's work. This book is dedicated to those people. The ones who have shared the laughs and frustrations with me on and off for the last thirty days. My hope is that this book has given some insight to my life as a groundskeeper and the everyday struggles of the common man.

POST SCRIPT

I T HAS BEEN nearly two years since
I finished putting pen to paper. I am
actually working as a grounds keeper at the same college in central Virginia
that I had left. In those two years, I have accumulated a ton of new stories. The
crazy boss is long gone. Maybe I should write a book!

Made in the USA
Lexington, KY
10 October 2017